A CONVERSATION WITH DARWIN

From Formation to Continuity:

Rethinking Human Existence

THEORY OF EVOLUTION
THEORY OF CONTINUITY

Dr. ADAM LUONG

To Aline, whose encouragement and belief have been the quiet strength behind every page of this work.

ACKNOWLEDGEMENTS

This book could not have been completed without the love, encouragement, and support of those closest to me.

First and foremost, I wish to thank my partner, Aline, whose presence has been the inspiration and motivation for me to reactivate my research. Her belief in me has sustained both my work and my spirit throughout this journey.

I am deeply grateful to Richard and Sylvia, who have been my dearest friends since the very beginning of my life in the United Kingdom. More than friends, they have become my family here, like an uncle and aunt who have stood beside me through every challenge. Their unwavering support, their kindness, and their generosity in proofreading my PhD thesis, this book, and the forthcoming ones, have been invaluable.

Last but never least, I owe heartfelt thanks to my second parents, Quang and Lien. Their care, guidance, and unconditional support have been a constant source of strength. They have given me not only encouragement but also the gift of a home.

To each of you, I extend my deepest gratitude. This work is as much yours as it is mine.

CONTENTS

PREFACE

When Charles Darwin published *On the Origin of Species* in 1859, he offered humanity a revolutionary lens through which to view itself. His Theory of Evolution by natural selection answered a profound question: *How did we come to be?*. It described the formation of life in terms of adaptation, variation, and survival, replacing centuries of speculation with a scientific framework that has endured for more than a century and a half. However, as transformative as Darwin's work was, it left another question largely untouched: *How do we continue to exist beyond the limits of a single lifetime?*

This book is not a critique of Darwin. It is a continuation of the conversation he began. Darwin's theory illuminated the mechanisms that shaped our bodies and species. My aim is to explore the structures that may allow aspects of our minds, identities, and symbolic capacities to persist beyond the lifespan of the individual organism. The Theory of Continuity, which originated from the Atomic Structure in Linguistics[1], proposes that certain cognitive and linguistic structures are not merely products of learning within one life, but are latent and enduring. These structures may re-emerge across generations, across cultures, and even across lives.

The idea for this book grew from two realisations. The first was that modern science, for all its remarkable advances, has yet

---

[1] Atomic Structure in Linguistics (ASL) was first introduced at the Postgraduate Research Showcase 2013 at the University of Southampton, where it received the Gold Award for new theory development. See Appendix C and D.

to explain convincingly the recurrence of highly specific knowledge, memories, or skills that appear in individuals without conventional transmission. The second was that my own theoretical work in linguistics, initially focused on the internal mechanics of meaning-making, seemed to intersect with this mystery in unexpected ways. In the Atomic Structure in Linguistics, meaning is built from fundamental semantic units that can cluster into stable configurations. These configurations can survive the loss of individual memory, remaining dormant until reactivated under certain conditions. Such a model opens the possibility of continuity in ways that Darwin's framework did not address.

Why Darwin, and why now? The answer lies in the enduring power of his method and his humility in the face of the unknown. Darwin did not pretend to have answered every question. Instead, he left space for the next stage of inquiry, confident that future thinkers would extend his work into new territories. Today, we find ourselves in an age of symbolic crisis, where questions of identity, meaning, and human purpose are as urgent as questions of genetic heritage were in the nineteenth century. It is in this moment that we must turn our attention from the origins of our form to the continuity of our being.

This book is, therefore, both an intellectual bridge and a proposal for a new paradigm. It begins with a recognition of what Darwin achieved and moves toward what he could not have imagined: a science of continuity. In the sections that follow, we will explore the mechanisms of formation and the structures of persistence, examine evidence from fields as diverse as Reincarnation research and Acquired Savant Syndrome, and outline how the Theory of Continuity may complement rather than replace the Theory of Evolution.

My hope is that this work will invite scientists, philosophers, linguists, and open-minded readers into a shared conversation about what it means to be human. If Darwin's legacy was to show that our existence has a history, then perhaps the legacy of the Theory of Continuity will be to show that our existence also has a future that is written into the very structure of who we are.

PART I - TWO BEGINNINGS
1. Introduction

Every great intellectual journey begins twice. The first beginning is the moment a question is asked with clarity for the very first time. The second beginning is when that same question is asked again in a new age, under new conditions, and is given a new kind of answer. Darwin's work represents the first beginning of the modern understanding of human existence. With *On the Origin of Species*[2], he brought together observation, reasoning, and the courage to challenge prevailing beliefs, offering an explanation for the formation of life that could be tested, debated, and refined. It was a beginning that altered the trajectory of science and the self-understanding of humanity.

No beginning is complete in itself. Every origin carries within it questions that remain unanswered. Darwin explained how life forms arise, adapt, and diversify, but his framework could not account for the persistence of certain aspects of human experience that appear to transcend a single lifetime. He addressed the body and its evolution, but not the continuity of mind, meaning, and identity. In the century and a half since his time, new evidence and new theoretical tools have emerged that invite us to consider another beginning. This second beginning asks how the human story continues beyond physical formation.

---

[2] Darwin, C. (1958). *On the Origin of Species*. New York: D.Appleton and Company. Available at: https://darwin-online.org.uk/converted/pdf/1861_OriginNY_F382.pdf. [Accessed 10th August 2025].

This second beginning is the starting point of the Theory of Continuity. It builds on the recognition that human existence is not only a matter of biological inheritance but also of structural persistence. Symbols, meanings, and cognitive patterns can endure without the direct transfer of DNA, reappearing in contexts far removed from their original appearance. This perspective does not reject Darwin's contribution. Rather, it extends into domains he could not have foreseen.

Part I introduces these two beginnings. It opens with an imagined correspondence across time, a letter written to Darwin from the present day, not in opposition but in continuation of his work. It then revisits the essentials of Darwin's explanation of formation, establishing the foundation on which the Theory of Continuity builds. Finally, it outlines how continuity operates as a structural principle, preparing the ground for the deeper explorations that will follow in the later parts of the book.

1.1 A Letter across Time

A conversation not of opposition, but of expansion

Dear Mr. Darwin,

I write to you not as a critic, but as a fellow inquirer, one who has been shaped by the intellectual courage you displayed in your time. Your work remains one of the most transformative achievements in human thought. You sought to understand life by looking deeply at the evidence before you, resisting the temptation to force nature into the patterns that convention demanded. By doing so, you gave us a language to speak of change, adaptation, and the long shaping of life over countless generations.

In reading your words, I am reminded that you never claimed to have solved every mystery. You wrote with caution, and with an honesty that left space for what you did not yet know. You gave us the story of our formation, but you also admitted that other questions lay beyond your reach. You observed life's variations, traced them to their roots in the struggle for existence, and saw the slow work of natural selection as the great sculptor of form. Yet the inner lives of beings, the continuity of what they know and remember, remained outside the scope of your theory.

I live in a different age, one that has inherited your insights but is faced with a new kind of puzzle. We now have tools to look at the brain in ways unimaginable in your day. We can map the regions that process language, memory, and emotion. We can watch neural networks change in response to experience. And yet, there remain moments when knowledge, skill, or memory appears in a person without the pathways that learning should require. We see children who speak of places they have never visited, name people long dead, and demonstrate abilities they have never been taught. We see sudden transformations in those who survive injury or illness, as if some hidden reservoir of capacity has been released.

Your work traced the origins of form to variation and inheritance within the body. Mine seeks to trace the persistence of certain structures of mind and meaning beyond the limits of one life. I call this the Theory of Continuity, and within it, the Atomic Structure in Linguistics. It begins from the observation that meaning is not an indivisible whole, but is built from small, fundamental units that can combine and recombine into stable patterns. These patterns, once formed, can survive the loss of individual memory. They can lie dormant until some trigger, such as an emotion, a context, or a sound, brings them again into expression.

If your theory showed that life is a history written in the body's language, mine suggests that there is also a history written in the language of the mind. These histories may move in parallel. They may even intertwine, yet they are not bound by the same limits. Biology tells us how the body survives and changes; structure may tell us how identity and meaning endure and return. I imagine you would meet these ideas with the same mixture of curiosity and caution that you applied to your own. Perhaps you would remind me, as you reminded your readers, that extraordinary claims require extraordinary evidence. I would agree, and in this book I will offer not speculation, but patterns and structures that can be examined, compared, and tested against the observations of many fields.

In writing to you, I am not trying to close the circle you began. Rather, I hope to draw a wider one that still contains your work. Just as you invited the thinkers of the future to extend your theory where it could not reach, I now invite those who read this to see our conversation as one that belongs not only to your century or mine, but to the enduring human effort to understand ourselves.

Yours across time,

Dr Adam Luong

1.2 Writing to Darwin from the Age of Symbolic Crisis

To write to Darwin today is to speak from an age that he could scarcely have imagined. The nineteenth century was a time of grand voyages, patient observation, and handwritten correspondence that carried ideas across oceans at the speed of wind and steam. It was also a time when language and meaning were relatively stable within cultural boundaries. Symbols evolved slowly, their transmission secured through oral traditions, printed books, and the shared assumptions of communities that were, for the most part, geographically and culturally distinct.

In the twenty-first century, that stability has fractured. We inhabit what can be called an age of symbolic crisis, a time in which the system of symbols, including words, images, and gestures through which we convey meaning, is no longer bound by fixed communities or gradual change. They travel instantly across the globe, often stripped from their original contexts and reshaped by forces that care little for continuity. In this environment, meanings can shift in days rather than decades. Entire systems of understanding can rise and collapse in a single generation.

This rapid transformation has profound consequences. If the body evolves through the slow accumulation of genetic changes, the symbolic life of humanity now evolves in a turbulent and accelerated cycle. The channels of communication that once preserved meaning have become the very means by which it can be unsettled. The result is a tension between the need for shared symbols and the constant redefinition of those symbols by competing narratives.

The crisis is not only one of speed and instability. It is also one of fragmentation. As digital networks and media create countless overlapping communities, each with its own lexicon and frames of reference, the possibility of a universal symbolic order diminishes. We live in an era where the same word or image can mean radically different things to different groups, and where the authority to define meaning is in constant dispute.

From the perspective of the Theory of Continuity, this symbolic crisis is not merely a challenge; it is also an opportunity. If certain structures of meaning are truly persistent, if they can survive the collapse of one symbolic order and emerge again in another, then this turbulence becomes a testing ground. In a world where so much is in flux, the reappearance of stable patterns can be observed more clearly. The age of symbolic crisis allows us to ask what in our symbolic life is ephemeral, and what endures beyond the moment.

Darwin studied life at a time when the pace of change allowed careful and sustained observation. His method required patient attention to small variations across generations. Our moment demands a different kind of observation, one that can detect persistent structures within the noise of constant change. Where Darwin looked for the gradual shaping of form, we must look for the recurrence of meaning across fractured symbolic landscapes.

It is in this context that the Theory of Continuity enters the conversation. By treating meaning as built from fundamental semantic units that can survive beyond the lifespan of an individual or the lifespan of a symbolic system, we gain a way to track the hidden stability beneath apparent chaos. Writing to Darwin from this age, I am telling him that the question he left unanswered, how human existence continues beyond formation, is no longer a matter for speculation. The evidence is all around us, in both the persistence of ancient structures and the strange reappearance of forgotten ones.

The symbolic crisis of our age is therefore not the end of continuity, but its most revealing stage. It forces us to look more deeply at the architecture of meaning, distinguishing what is temporary from what is structurally inevitable. In this, Darwin's spirit of inquiry remains our guide, urging us to examine the evidence patiently, even in a time that moves with unsettling speed.

2. How We Were Formed

Any attempt to understand continuity must first address the question of formation. Before we can speak of persistence, recurrence, or the reactivation of structure, we must consider how that structure came into being in the first place. For Darwin, the formation of species was a matter of gradual change shaped by variation, inheritance, and the relentless pressures of natural selection. The forms we see in nature are the outcome of countless generations in which some traits were preserved and others were lost.

It is, therefore, worth examining the foundations that Darwin's work laid for thinking about human origins. It also considers the boundaries of his theory, recognising that while it accounts for the emergence of physical forms, it does not fully encompass the emergence of structures of meaning. If biology can describe how the body came to be, it is less equipped to explain how the architecture of thought, language, and symbolic identity took shape.

In exploring these questions, the section moves between two levels of analysis. The first is the biological level, which situates human beings within the broader web of life. The second is the structural level, which considers the formation of the symbolic systems that define human culture and consciousness. Both are necessary to understand the conditions in which continuity can operate.

By tracing the pathways from physical formation to the beginnings of structural organisation, this section sets the stage for the central argument of the book. It invites the reader to see human origins not as a single completed event in the distant past, but as the opening chapter in an ongoing story, a story in which the forces that shaped our bodies also prepared the ground for the persistence of meaning.

2.1 Natural Selection and Genetic Inheritance

The story of human formation begins with the body. It begins with cells, with the intricate machinery of life that replicates and modifies itself through countless generations. Darwin's central insight was that the diversity of life is not fixed, but is shaped by gradual changes in heritable traits, guided by the pressures of survival and reproduction. In his time, the mechanism of inheritance was not fully understood. The structure of DNA had not yet been discovered, and the science of genetics was still in its infancy. Yet his observations of variation, competition, and adaptation formed a coherent framework that explained how species arise and diverge.

Natural selection is a simple yet profound process. Within any population, individuals differ in ways that affect their ability to survive and reproduce. Those whose traits give them an advantage in a given environment are more likely to pass those traits on to their offspring. Over many generations, these advantageous traits become more common, and the population changes. This process does not follow a predetermined path. It is shaped by the interplay between chance variation and the demands of the environment. It is at once methodical and unpredictable, creative and constrained.

The later discovery of genes and the double helix structure of DNA provided the molecular explanation for what Darwin had described from observation. Genes are units of information encoded in the sequence of nucleotides, and they direct the synthesis of proteins that shape the body's structure and function. Variation arises through mutation, recombination, and other processes, ensuring that no two individuals are genetically identical, except in the case of identical twins. Genetic inheritance became the material basis for Darwin's conceptual framework, confirming that life's diversity is the result of both random change and systematic selection.

For Darwin, the focus was on the physical form. His theory could account for the length of a finch's beak, the colour of a moth's wings, or the musculature of a predator. It could explain why some traits persisted while others vanished, why a species might flourish in one environment and disappear in another. His work gave humanity a map of its own physical origins, a way to trace the human body's features back through the branching paths of evolutionary history.

However, even as Darwin offered an explanation for the shaping of form, he acknowledged that the question of mind was far more complex. The origin of consciousness, the capacity for language, and the intricacies of symbolic thought lay beyond what his theory could fully capture. He recognised that mental life was somehow rooted in the physical, yet he could not map its inheritance with the same clarity as he could for physical traits.

2.2 What Darwin Solved and What He Could not Reach

Darwin's achievement was not simply that he described a mechanism for change in living beings. It was that he provided a unifying principle that linked the smallest details of life's variation to the grand patterns of its history. Before *On the Origin of Species*, explanations for the diversity of life were often fragmented, speculative, or rooted in fixed doctrines. Darwin brought them together under a single explanatory framework: natural selection acting on inherited variation over vast spans of time.

He solved the problem of *how* living forms emerge, adapt, and diversify without invoking external design or immutable categories. His theory showed that complex adaptations could arise gradually from simple beginnings, provided there was enough time and a consistent mechanism for filtering which variations endured. He demonstrated that species are not static but dynamic, capable of diverging from a common ancestor to produce the astonishing variety we see today.

By rooting change in the interaction between variation and environmental pressures, Darwin also explained why no species is perfectly adapted, and why life is in a constant state of flux. His work accounted for both the fine-tuned fit between organism and environment, and the imperfections that inevitably remain when conditions change faster than forms can adjust. In doing so, he reframed humanity's place in nature. We were no longer set apart by a special creation, but were kin to all living things, shaped by the same forces that sculpted every other species.

The very strength of Darwin's theory, however, also defined its boundaries. Natural selection explains the transmission of traits through biological reproduction, but it does so in material terms. It depends on the passage of genetic information encoded in the physical structures of the body. This makes it an exceptionally powerful framework for understanding anatomy, physiology, and behaviour that can be tied to heritable variation. But it leaves untouched any phenomena that do not clearly follow the path of genetic inheritance.

Darwin's theory could not fully address the origins or persistence of symbolic systems, such as language, myth, or abstract knowledge. It could not explain how certain patterns of thought or fragments of experience sometimes appear without the direct learning processes that would ordinarily be required. It offered no mechanism for how a skill, an image, or a set of words could recur in an individual who had never been exposed to them in this lifetime.

In fairness to Darwin, these questions were not only beyond his evidence; they were also beyond the conceptual tools available in his time. Without the modern study of neurolinguistics, memory structures, or cross-cultural symbolic systems, there was little basis on which to explore such possibilities. His own writings reveal that he was cautious when discussing the human mind. He recognised its complexity, but he viewed it primarily as an advanced product of the same evolutionary processes that produced the physical form.

Yet history shows that Darwin was aware of the limits of his framework. His correspondence and later works reveal a readiness to acknowledge gaps and an expectation that future science would venture into areas he could not. He left space for new kinds of inheritance to be discovered, though he could not predict their form.

It is in this space that the Theory of Continuity takes root. The unexplained reappearance of structured knowledge, the recurrence of certain symbolic patterns, and the persistence of identity-like elements beyond a single lifespan are not contradictions of Darwin's theory, but phenomena it was never designed to address. Darwin mapped the evolution of the body. What remains is to map the continuity of the mind and meaning.

2.3 A Model of Physical Origin

From Darwin's work, we inherit a model of physical origin that is both elegant and robust. It begins with the observation that variation exists within every population of living things. No two individuals are identical, and these differences, however small, may influence an organism's ability to survive and reproduce. This variation is the raw material upon which natural selection operates.

The process unfolds in a sequence that, while simple in outline, is vast in scope. Variation in traits arises from changes in the hereditary material. In Darwin's day, the underlying causes of variation were unknown. Today, we understand that such changes can result from mutations in the DNA sequence, from the recombination of genes during reproduction, and from other molecular processes that introduce novelty into the genetic code. These variations are then tested in the context of the environment, which presents a shifting array of challenges and opportunities.

Those traits that increase the likelihood of survival and reproduction are more likely to be passed to the next generation. Over many generations, the accumulation of these advantageous traits reshapes the population. Gradual change over long periods can result in the formation of new species, while unfavourable traits tend to disappear as their carriers leave fewer descendants. This mechanism is not a directed or purposeful process. It does not anticipate future needs or design optimal solutions. Rather, it is a constant filtering process that retains what works well enough to persist and discards what does not.

The later discovery of the structure of DNA and the principles of molecular genetics provided the missing link in Darwin's model. We now know that genes, encoded in the sequence of nucleotides within the DNA molecule, carry the instructions for building and maintaining the organism. These instructions are expressed through the production of proteins, which perform the structural and regulatory roles essential to life. This understanding gave Darwin's theory a molecular foundation, confirming that biological inheritance is a physical process carried in the body's microscopic architecture.

In this model of origin, inheritance is strictly material. Traits are passed from one generation to the next through the replication and transmission of genetic material. The organism's body, with all its capacities and limitations, is shaped by the interplay between inherited instructions and environmental pressures. Evolution is, in this sense, the history of form written in the language of DNA.

The success of this model is evident in its explanatory power. It accounts for the distribution of traits in populations, the patterns observed in the fossil record, and the complex adaptations seen in every branch of the tree of life. It explains why related species share physical features, why isolated populations diverge, and why organisms are often perfectly suited to their environments, yet never perfectly fixed. It provides the framework for disciplines as diverse as ecology, paleontology, and modern medicine, all of which depend on understanding how living forms arise and change.

However, this model has clear boundaries. It does not account for the inheritance of structures that are not embedded in the physical genome. It cannot, by its own principles, explain the persistence of meaning, identity, or knowledge that is not carried by genetic material. It assumes that what is inherited is what is physically encoded, and that the death of the body marks the end of its contribution to the evolutionary process.

To move from the formation of the body to the continuity of the mind requires an extension of this model into a new domain. Just as Darwin's theory explained the evolution of anatomy and physiology, another framework is needed to explain the persistence and re-emergence of symbolic and cognitive structures. This is the task of the Theory of Continuity. It does not reject the model of physical origin, but builds upon it, recognising that the story of human existence is not complete if told only in terms of the body's evolution. The next step is to show that formation is only one part of a larger process, and that continuity is the other.

3. How We Exist Continuously

Darwin's model of formation explains the evolution of the body through natural selection and genetic inheritance. It accounts for the way physical traits are passed from generation to generation, shaped by the demands of the environment and the pressures of survival. However, human existence is not contained entirely within the body. We are also defined by our thoughts, our memories, our languages, our symbolic systems, and our sense of identity. These aspects are not inscribed directly in the sequence of our DNA. They belong to another layer of reality that interacts with, but is not confined to, the biological framework.

The Theory of Continuity begins with recognising that these non-biological aspects of human life can persist independently of the body. They are not mystical or supernatural in nature. Rather, they are structured patterns of meaning and identity that can be retained, transmitted, and reactivated even when the original physical medium has ceased to exist. The study of this kind of persistence requires a different lens from the one Darwin used for formation. It is a lens focused on structure, memory, and symbolic recurrence rather than solely on genes and anatomy.

3.1 Structural Survival beyond Biology

Structural survival is the continuation of organised patterns of meaning, knowledge, and identity outside the limits of a single physical lifetime. The term does not imply that the biological organism survives. Instead, it refers to the endurance of the structural configuration of meaning itself.

To understand this idea, it helps to distinguish between the medium and the pattern it carries. In genetics, the medium is the DNA molecule, and the pattern is the arrangement of nucleotides that determines the traits of the organism. In the realm of meaning, the medium may be a human brain, a symbolic tradition, a cultural artefact, or an interpersonal exchange. The pattern in this case is the arrangement of the smallest units of meaning, which I call *semantic atoms*. These combine into clusters called *semantic cores*, which are then expressed in various forms such as speech, gesture, art, or ritual.

What is important is that a pattern can survive even when the medium changes. A piece of music can be played on a piano, a violin, or a computer-generated instrument, yet remain recognisably the same melody. Similarly, a configuration of semantic atoms can be reconstructed in a new mind, in a new life, without direct teaching. It may arise in a child who displays knowledge or skill beyond their learning history, or in an artist who suddenly expresses symbolic motifs found in distant cultures.

The persistence of such patterns suggests that structural survival operates in a domain parallel to, but not dependent on, genetic inheritance. This is not a rejection of the biological model, but an extension of it into the symbolic and cognitive realm.

3.2 Memory, Trauma, and Symbolic Loops

Memory is not a simple archive of past experiences. It is a living system that continually reshapes itself. Some memories fade or become distorted, while others grow stronger through repetition and emotional reinforcement. Among the strongest and most enduring are those associated with trauma. Traumatic experiences are often encoded with an intensity that makes them resistant to erasure. The emotions tied to them create deep impressions that are difficult to alter.

When such memories form strong emotional associations, they can generate what I call *symbolic loops*. A symbolic loop is a recurring cycle in which a particular image, phrase, gesture, or idea triggers an emotional response. That emotional response then strengthens the memory of the original pattern, making it more likely to be recalled again. Over time, the loop can function independently of the original event. The symbolic pattern becomes self-sustaining, existing as a structure that does not require constant reinforcement from new experiences.

Symbolic loops can operate within a single lifetime, but the Theory of Continuity suggests they can also span lifetimes. If certain structural patterns are capable of surviving the end of the biological medium, then the emotional charge that sustains them may help carry them forward into a new context. This could explain why some individuals display intense emotional reactions to stimuli they have never encountered before, or why certain fears, affinities, or aversions appear without an identifiable cause in the current life.

The interaction between memory and emotion is therefore central to the understanding of continuity. It shows how structures can become stable enough to survive disconnection from their original context, and how they can re-emerge when conditions align to trigger their expression.

3.3 Introducing the Theory of Continuity

3.3.1. The Need for a New Framework

For centuries, scholars and lay observers alike have struggled with phenomena that appear to resist the boundaries of conventional explanation. Children who recall past lives with uncanny precision, adults who acquire extraordinary abilities after brain injury, and individuals who display inexplicable emotional responses to places or people all raise the same underlying question: *how can knowledge and memory persist beyond the limits of biological inheritance and cultural teaching?* Traditional accounts often fall into one of two unsatisfying extremes. On the one hand, mystical or religious explanations invoke the soul, Reincarnation, or divine intervention. On the other hand, scientific explanations rooted solely in genetics or neurological chance fail to account for the patterned and meaningful recurrence of these experiences. What is needed is a model that is at once structural, empirical, and open to the complexities of lived human experience.

The Theory of Continuity, grounded in the Atomic Structure in Linguistics (ASL), is offered as such a model. It does not invoke metaphysical essences, nor does it reduce phenomena to chance anomalies of the brain. Instead, it proposes that meaning itself has a structure, and that this structure can survive, reconfigure, and re-emerge across different lifetimes and contexts. ASL offers a comprehensive framework for understanding how meaning is organised, preserved, and reactivated beyond the temporal boundaries of a single human life. It begins with the recognition that meaning is not simply a fluid, formless quality of human cognition, but is instead structured, layered, and governed by identifiable principles. These principles enable patterns of knowledge, symbolism, and skill to survive the passing of an individual and re-emerge when the right conditions arise.

3.3.2. The Elements of the Theory

At the foundation of the model are four interrelated components.

Semantic Atoms

At its foundation lies the concept of Semantic Atoms. These are the smallest and irreducible units of meaning, distinct from words or sounds, yet fundamental in shaping how we perceive and communicate. A semantic atom is not a fixed symbol but a dynamic element that may take shape through concept, action, emotion, or experience. These four modalities orbit an Invisible Core, which represents the essence of meaning that cannot be directly expressed but continuously influences how atoms emerge.

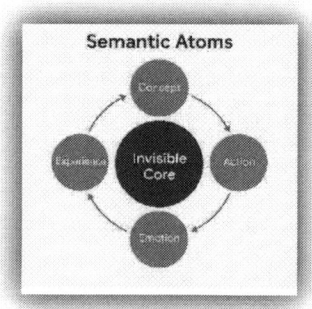

Individually, atoms hold potential but have limited expressive power. For example, the term "mother" may differ across languages, yet at its root lies a stable semantic atom: the nurturer–child relation. A child who unexpectedly utters "maa" in an unfamiliar tongue may not be recalling vocabulary, but surfacing the atomic unit of maternal relation. In this way, semantic atoms provide the building blocks that combine into larger structures of memory and meaning.

Semantic Cores

Semantic cores are clusters of semantic atoms that bond together around a shared theme. Atoms do not cluster randomly; they join through specific bonding mechanisms. Thematic congruence draws atoms into relation when they share a common field of meaning. Emotional resonance stabilises these bonds by infusing them with affective intensity. Frequency of co-activation strengthens connections over time, as repeated association reinforces the cluster.

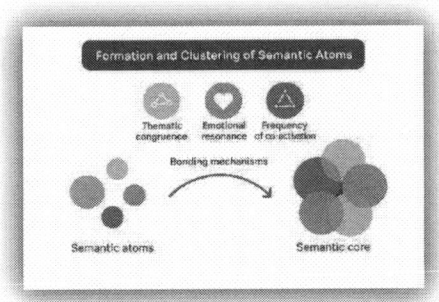

Once formed, these clusters become semantic cores, which are deeper organisations of meaning that act as reservoirs of structured memory. They hold patterns of concept, emotion, action, and experience in an integrated form, allowing them to persist across time and context even when not actively expressed.

A distinctive property of cores is what may be called semantic gravity. Some cores exert a stronger pull than others, drawing additional atoms into their orbit and increasing their likelihood of reappearing across contexts or even lifetimes. A core bound up with family roles, emotional attachments, or symbolic rituals may possess far greater stability than one linked to trivial or fleeting experiences. Semantic gravity explains why certain memories, skills, or predispositions endure with remarkable clarity, while others dissolve into obscurity.

Contextual Membrane

Surrounding each core is a *Contextual Membrane*, which functions as the filters that regulate how cores are expressed. Culture, syntax, environment, and situational factors shape the porosity of these membranes. In some contexts, a semantic core may leak through only faintly, while in others it may flood expression with striking clarity.

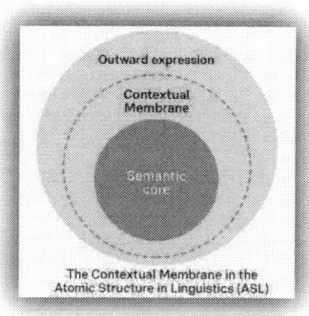

At one level lies the *syntactic layer*, which governs how meanings are arranged and articulated within a linguistic or symbolic system. At another level lies the *situational layer*, which incorporates the immediate environment, cultural norms, and relational dynamics that either inhibit or encourage expression.

The porosity of these layers varies: in some contexts, the membrane is thin and allows a semantic core to emerge with little distortion, while in others it is thick and only partial fragments can pass through. By recognising these layers, we can understand why the same underlying structure may manifest as fluent recall in one setting, as confused fragments in another, or remain completely latent until triggered.

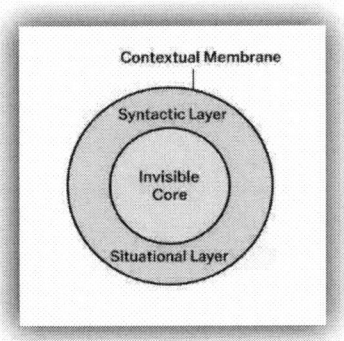

Contextual membranes are not uniform. They may be *thin*, allowing cores to pass into expression with relative ease, or *thick*, restricting expression to faint fragments. For example, a thin membrane might allow a child to blurt out a memory, whereas a thick one would filter it into vague impressions. They may also be *homogeneous*, applying a consistent filter across contexts, or *inhomogeneous*, varying in permeability depending on emotional, cultural, or environmental conditions. For instance, a child in India might openly describe past-life memories in a receptive family (thin membrane), whereas a child in the West might only produce vague drawings or nightmares (thick, inhomogeneous membrane). These variations account for why a memory or skill may be vividly expressed in one domain, such as music, yet remain inaccessible in another, such as language.

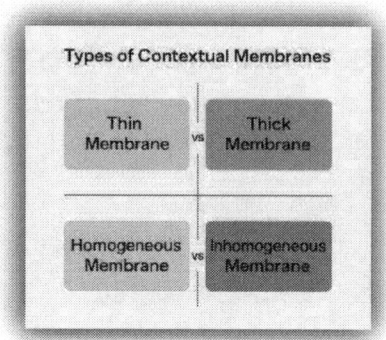

Visiblers

The visibler manifestations of these cores are called *Visiblers*. These are the observable behaviours, words, gestures, or artistic expressions through which the underlying structure of meaning becomes apparent. When a child sketches a ship they have never seen or a musician improvises a melody with no formal training, these acts are visiblers which are the visible manifestations of underlying cores. They are not the structure itself, but its surface echoes.

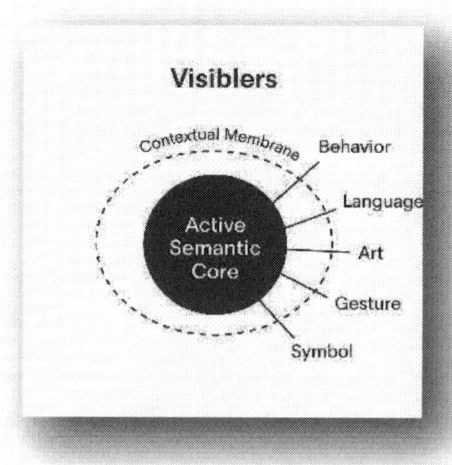

A distinctive feature of the Theory of Continuity is its explanation of *dormancy* and *reactivation*. Semantic cores may remain inactive for years, even across generations or lifetimes, yet under certain conditions, the contextual membrane becomes permeable enough for the core to re-emerge. This reactivation may be triggered by emotional resonance, environmental similarity, symbolic repetition, or a precise combination of stimuli that reconstructs the original context. When this occurs, the individual manifests visiblers that reveal a structural continuity with a previous state of knowledge or identity, even if no conventional transmission such as teaching or direct exposure has taken place.

This structural model reframes continuity as a scientifically investigable phenomenon rather than a purely philosophical or metaphysical speculation. Just as the principles of chemistry dictate that hydrogen and oxygen will bond to form water under specific conditions, the principles of meaning-making dictate that certain configurations of semantic atoms will reliably reassemble when the right symbolic and cognitive conditions are met. This explains why a child may display knowledge of a language or cultural practice never encountered in their current life, or why individuals recovering from brain trauma can suddenly demonstrate advanced artistic or mathematical ability without prior training.

3.3.3. The Dynamic Process

The elements of the Theory of Continuity do not exist in isolation. They form a dynamic system in which semantic atoms, semantic cores, visiblers, and contextual membranes constantly interact. Understanding this process is crucial because it is through these interactions that continuity across lives, traumas, or cultural settings becomes possible.

At the beginning of the process are *semantic atoms*, which function as sparks of meaning. By themselves, they may appear fragmented, but they rarely remain detached. Over time, they cluster into *semantic cores*, which give these fragments coherence and stability. The process of clustering is not random but guided by the gravitational pull of certain themes and experiences. For instance, atoms related to kinship, place, or symbolic ritual often consolidate into particularly durable cores because of their emotional weight and existential relevance.

Once formed, semantic cores seek expression. They can only become visible through *visiblers*, the outward manifestations in speech, writing, gesture, music, drawing, or behaviour. A core related to spatial memory, for example, may emerge as a child's ability to navigate an unfamiliar town, or as an adult's untrained but precise skill in cartographic drawing. In each case, the visibler offers a partial window into the deeper structure of the core.

The appearance of visibler, however, is never automatic. It is shaped by the *contextual membranes* that surround and filter the process of expression. Membranes consist of layers that regulate expression on multiple levels, from syntactic ordering to situational appropriateness. They also vary in type, sometimes thin and porous, sometimes thick and resistant, sometimes consistent, sometimes variable across settings. When a membrane is highly porous, a semantic core may be expressed with startling clarity, as when a savant produces complex musical compositions without training. When the membrane is dense, expression may appear in faint fragments, such as a fleeting sense of déjà vu or a half-remembered word in an unknown language.

The process is therefore cyclical and adaptive. Semantic atoms feed into cores, cores press outward through membranes, and visibler become the observable forms that, in turn, may reinforce or reshape the core itself. In some instances, an expressed visibler deepens the gravitational strength of a core, making it more likely to persist or re-emerge later. In other instances, contextual resistance may suppress expression, allowing the core to remain latent until conditions shift.

This dynamic is not limited to a single lifetime. It is precisely this structural interplay that makes continuity possible. Cores with high semantic gravity may survive dissolution, their atoms reassembling in a new host and pressing again for expression. The outcome, whether in Reincarnation cases or Acquired Savant Syndrome, is not a mystical transference but the structural persistence of meaning across time and circumstance.

The Theory of Continuity does not seek to displace Darwin's Theory of Evolution, but to complement it by addressing an entirely different domain: the evolution and persistence of symbolic and cognitive structures. Where evolution charts the transformation of physical forms through genetic inheritance, the Theory of Continuity maps the endurance and reappearance of mental and symbolic architectures through structural inheritance. Together, these perspectives form a more complete account of human existence, one that acknowledges both the adaptive journey of the body and the enduring journey of the mind.

By situating meaning within a structured, transmissible framework, the Theory of Continuity not only deepens our understanding of memory, identity, and creativity but also opens the door to new methods of research that transcend disciplinary boundaries. It invites linguistics, neuroscience, anthropology, psychology, and even artificial intelligence to collaborate in exploring the architectures of continuity, an exploration that may ultimately redefine how we understand the survival and transformation of human knowledge.

PART II - WHAT DARWIN MISSED

Darwin gave the modern world a coherent account of how living forms are shaped by variation, selection, and inheritance. His framework explained the emergence of species, the adaptation of organisms to their environments, and the slow transformation of life over vast stretches of time. However, for all its explanatory power, his theory was not complete. It was not intended to be. Darwin worked within the limits of the evidence available to him, and he was careful to confine his conclusions to what could be supported by observation. He acknowledged that there were areas of human existence that his model could not reach.

One of those areas is the persistence of meaning, identity, and symbolic structure beyond the lifespan of the individual. Darwin could explain how the body is formed, but not how certain patterns of thought, memory, or symbolic association seem to endure without genetic transmission. His theory was grounded in the biology of form; it did not have the conceptual tools to address the continuity of mind.

The discussion now begins where Darwin's reach ended. It explores the domain of symbolic and cognitive inheritance, which is a form of continuity operating outside the mechanisms of DNA. In this domain, the environment is not defined by climate or predation, but by the total field of lived experience: relationships, cultural symbols, language systems, and emotional landscapes. Here, the selective forces are not purely physical, but affective and symbolic.

The sections that follow will examine how meaning is preserved and reactivated across time. They will show why certain patterns endure while others vanish, how trauma and emotion shape the architecture of being, and why the Theory of Continuity provides a necessary complement to Darwin's theory of formation. This is not an attempt to replace Darwin's work, but to extend it into a domain he recognised as important but did not attempt to map.

If Part I established the two beginnings: the formation of the body and the continuity of the mind, then Part II focuses on the gap between them. It is within this gap that much of human experience resides, and it is here that we must look to find the structures that Darwin could not see, but which shape the ongoing story of human existence.

4. There is No Gene for Memory

When we speak of memory, it is tempting to imagine that somewhere within our DNA lies a code that directly stores the details of our experiences. Since genes are the building blocks of heredity, it might seem reasonable to assume that memories themselves could be carried in genetic form and transmitted with the same reliability as eye colour or blood type. In popular discourse, phrases such as "it runs in the family" or "born with the gift" often blur the distinction between biological inheritance and cognitive capacity. Yet, when examined scientifically, the idea that there is a single gene, or even a set of genes, for memory quickly unravels.

Modern genetics has shown that DNA provides the blueprint for proteins, enzymes, and structural elements that make up the living body. It sets the parameters within which the nervous system can develop, but it does not inscribe specific experiences. Unlike a digital storage system, the genome [3]does not contain entries for childhood songs, faces of loved ones, or the texture of grief. Instead, memory emerges from dynamic processes in the brain, from patterns of neural connectivity and activity that are shaped by interaction with the environment. In other words, genes prepare the stage upon which memory may unfold, but they do not script the play.

---

[3] A genome is the complete set of DNA (or in some viruses, RNA) in an organism, containing all the instructions needed to build and maintain that organism.

Neuroscience confirms this distinction. Studies of synaptic plasticity demonstrate that memory is the result of strengthening or weakening connections between neurons in response to activity. Long-term potentiation, the best-studied mechanism of memory formation, illustrates how repeated activation of neural circuits enhances their responsiveness. This is not the result of a single gene dictating recall but of networks reorganising themselves in ways that encode patterns of experience. What we remember is embedded not in DNA but in the ever-changing architecture of neural communication.

Still, the story does not end here. The emergence of epigenetics has complicated the picture by showing that life experiences can indeed influence the regulation of genes. Trauma, nutrition, or environmental stressors can alter gene expression through chemical modifications such as methylation[4]. These changes may even be passed on to the next generation, producing what is sometimes called "transgenerational inheritance[5]." At first glance, this might appear to vindicate the idea of a "memory gene." However, what epigenetics preserves is not the memory of a specific event but rather the structural readiness of the organism to respond in particular ways. For example, the descendants of individuals exposed to famine may show altered metabolic responses, but they do not recall the famine itself. Likewise, the child of a

---

[4] Methylation is the biochemical process of transferring a methyl group (a carbon and three hydrogen atoms) to a molecule, such as DNA, proteins, or RNA.

[5] Transgenerational inheritance is the passing of acquired characteristics, not from DNA mutation, but through epigenetic mechanisms from one generation to the next, often in response to environmental factors.

traumatised parent may inherit heightened stress reactivity, but not the detailed images of the traumatic event.

It is here that the Theory of Continuity makes its intervention. If biology provides an explanation for origin, structure provides an explanation for recurrence. The persistence of memory across lifetimes or through traumatic awakening cannot be accounted for by a genetic model of inheritance. Instead, what continues is not the physical inscription of events but the re-emergence of structural patterns of meaning. These patterns, what I call semantic atoms and semantic cores, are preserved not in DNA but in the latent architectures of cognition and culture. They reassemble when the right conditions arise, much as a melody can be played again when the notes are struck in sequence, even if no single instrument permanently holds the tune.

This reframing allows us to see why certain memories and skills can appear without prior learning. In cases of Acquired Savant Syndrome, for instance, musical or mathematical abilities surface after brain injury, despite the individual never having trained in those domains. Genes cannot explain this sudden emergence of highly specific knowledge. Neural reorganisation alone cannot explain why the content has coherence, symbolic density, or thematic resonance. What the Theory of Continuity offers is an account of how latent semantic cores, preserved structurally rather than genetically, can be reactivated when barriers are removed or new neural pathways provide access.

Moreover, this framework clarifies the difference between potential and content. Genes provide the potential, the capacity to form a brain capable of memory. Structure provides content, the specific clusters of meaning that persist and reappear. This distinction is vital. A genetic model of memory risks reducing human identity to a sequence of nucleotides[6], while a structural model preserves the richness of lived experience and symbolic recurrence.

In the broader scientific debate, this perspective also bridges a gap that has long existed between neuroscience and the humanities. Neuroscience explains how synapses fire and networks change. The humanities study how symbols, narratives, and cultural meanings endure. The Theory of Continuity situates memory at the intersection of these domains. It proposes that memory is neither a material object stored in genes nor a purely cultural artefact, but a structured phenomenon: an organised architecture of meaning capable of recurrence.

Recent findings in cognitive science lend support to this view. Research into "engrams[7]," the physical traces of memory in the brain[8], shows that memories are distributed across networks rather than localised in a single site. Similarly, experiments on reconsolidation[9] reveal that each act of recall is also an act of

---

[6] Nucleotides are the basic building blocks of DNA and RNA, consisting of a phosphate group, a pentose sugar (deoxyribose for DNA or ribose for RNA), and a nitrogenous base (A, G, C, and T for DNA; A, G, C, and U for RNA).

[7] An engram is a theoretical physical representation of a memory in the brain, consisting of the enduring biophysical or biochemical changes in a network of neurons that have been activated by a past experience.

[8] Josselyn, S. & Tonegawa, S. (2020) Memory engrams: Recalling the past and imagining the future. *PubMed Central*, 3;367(6473):eaaw4325. Available at: https://pmc.ncbi.nlm.nih.gov/articles/PMC7577560/. [Accessed 19 August 2025].

[9] Nader, K. (2015) Reconsolidation and dynamic nature of memory. *PubMed Central*, 7(10): a021782. Available at: https://pmc.ncbi.nlm.nih.gov/articles/PMC4588064/. [Accessed 19 August 2025].

reconstruction. Memory is never simply replayed but reassembled, which is why it can evolve, distort, or resurface in unexpected contexts. If memory is inherently reconstructive, then it makes sense to think of it as structural rather than genetic: a set of rules for reactivation rather than a static inscription.

The implications of this shift are profound. It suggests that what we inherit across generations is not the specific content of our parents' lives but the structural configurations that organise meaning. This explains both the resilience of cultural symbols and the recurrence of themes in individual lives. It also provides a framework for understanding extraordinary cases such as Reincarnation narratives, where children report memories of previous lives with striking specificity, or Acquired Savant Syndrome, where abilities emerge suddenly and without conventional training. These are not anomalies to be dismissed as mystical but structural reactivations that reveal the architecture of continuity.

Therefore, to say there is no gene for memory is not to deny the biological foundation of cognition. It is to recognise the limits of genetics in explaining phenomena of recurrence and continuity. The genome builds the body, but structure preserves meaning. DNA writes the possibility of a brain, but the Theory of Continuity explains why symbolic patterns outlast that brain's individual lifespan. Biology explains how life begins; structure explains how meaning returns.

4.1 Inheritance of Symbols versus DNA

The question of whether memory could be passed down biologically has occupied scientific, philosophical, and cultural debates for centuries. In the nineteenth century, Lamarckian notions of acquired characteristics[10] suggested that what was learned in one lifetime could be biologically transmitted to the next. Darwin himself did not fully endorse Lamarckism, but he remained open to the idea of pangenesis[11], a speculative model in which "gemmules" circulating in the body could encode acquired traits. With the discovery of DNA in the mid-twentieth century, enthusiasm grew that heredity might explain not only physical traits but also the transmission of memory. Some popular science writing even speculated about a gene for memory or a gene for intelligence, as if complex symbolic repertoires could be reduced to molecular sequences.

Despite decades of intensive research in genetics and neuroscience, no such memory gene has ever been discovered. Genes, as contemporary biology makes clear, encode proteins and regulate the development of neural structures, but they do not directly carry experiential content. The genome can predispose an organism toward certain capacities such as musical aptitude, linguistic sensitivity, or rapid neural plasticity. Yet it does not transmit specific songs, languages, or symbolic

---

[10] Britannica (n.d.) *Lamarkism*. Available at:
https://www.britannica.com/science/Lamarckism/Persistence-of-Lamarckism. [Accessed 19 August 2025].

[11] Pangenesis, proposed by Charles Darwin, was a theory of heredity suggesting that all cells in an organism shed tiny particles called "gemmules" that carry information to the reproductive organs and are then passed on to offspring, potentially explaining the inheritance of acquired characteristics. While largely discredited, it's now seen as a precursor to modern genetics.

frameworks. Neuroscience reinforces this point. Eric Kandel's Nobel Prize-winning research [12]on memory formation in Aplysia demonstrated that memory involves synaptic modifications, cascades of neurotransmitters, and structural changes in neural circuits. These changes are emergent properties of neural activity rather than instructions written into DNA. Memory, therefore, belongs to the dynamic level of neurocognitive structure, not the static code of genes.

The persistence of the memory gene idea led to several reformulations. In the 1960s, experiments on memory transfer through RNA injections in planaria[13] raised hopes that biochemical molecules could encode learned behaviors. These studies were later discredited as irreproducible or flawed in methodology. More recent research in epigenetics[14] has revealed that environmental conditions can alter the way genes are expressed, creating transgenerational effects. For example, stress or trauma can modify methylation patterns, and some of these modifications can be passed to offspring. While intriguing, these findings concern predispositions in affect and physiology rather than the inheritance of symbolic knowledge. They do not explain why a child might spontaneously recognise rituals, places, or languages beyond their immediate experience.

It is at this point that the Theory of Continuity makes its contribution. Biological inheritance provides the scaffolding for

---

[12] The Nobel Prize (2000). *Eric Kandel*. Available at:
https://www.nobelprize.org/prizes/medicine/2000/kandel/facts/. [Accessed 20 August 2025].

[13] Greenspan, R. J. (2003). RNA and Memory: From Feeding to Localization. *Current Biology*, 13(4), pp.R126-R127. Available at:
https://www.sciencedirect.com/science/article/pii/S096098220300071X. [Accessed 20 August 2025].

[14] The Institute of Cancer Research (2023). New Study Unveil Epigenetic 'traffic lights' Controlling Stop and Go for Gene Activity. Available at: https://www.icr.ac.uk/about-us/icr-news/detail/new-study-unveils-epigenetic-traffic-lights-controlling-stop-and-go-for-gene-activity

cognition, equipping the human organism with a brain capable of learning, storing, and reactivating knowledge. The symbolic architectures that define human experience, which the theory describes as semantic atoms, are not reducible to genetic material. They belong to a structural domain that transcends molecular transmission. Just as the laws of mathematics are not encoded in the genetic sequence but remain accessible to any mind capable of symbolic reasoning, semantic atoms persist as latent structures of meaning that can re-emerge across contexts and lifetimes.

The distinction between genetic and symbolic inheritance becomes clear when we examine the irregularity of symbolic transmission. If DNA carried the content of memory, all children within the same lineage would inherit identical symbolic repertoires. In reality, we see discontinuous but striking manifestations. A child may recall a language they were never taught. A painter may produce works in the style of a master they have never encountered. A musician may, after a brain injury, play with technical fluency that was absent from their earlier life. These phenomena resist genetic explanation but align with the principle that meaning persists in latent structural form and can be reactivated when conditions are favourable.

The inheritance of symbols diverges fundamentally from the inheritance of DNA. DNA ensures the survival and reproduction of biological organisms. Semantic atoms ensure the survival and recurrence of meaning. Genes build bodies while structures of continuity build symbolic worlds. To conflate the two is to mistake the material substrate for the architecture of experience. Biology provides the explanation for origin, while structure provides the explanation for recurrence. Together, they form parallel systems of inheritance, one material and one symbolic, each indispensable to the unfolding of human life.

4.2 Semantic Atoms and Non-Biological Transmission

The Theory of Continuity begins with the idea that meaning is built from the smallest indivisible units, which I call semantic atoms. Each semantic atom carries a minimal unit of meaning, just as a chemical atom carries the smallest stable unit of a chemical element. These semantic atoms combine to form semantic cores, which are complex patterns of meaning that have stability and coherence.

If DNA transmits the biological codes of life, then semantic atoms transmit the symbolic codes of meaning. Unlike genes, semantic atoms are not material sequences located in chromosomes[15]. They are the smallest irreducible units of meaning, fragments of symbolic order that can cluster into semantic cores and then find outward expression in visiblers. Their persistence does not depend on genetic continuity but on structural recurrence, which explains why memories, languages, or symbolic associations can reappear across individuals, contexts, and even lifetimes without the mediation of direct teaching.

Non-biological transmission of meaning is not a new idea. Philosophers have long recognised the possibility that knowledge and symbolic systems endure independently of their material

---

[15] Chromosomes are tightly packaged bundles of DNA found in the nucleus of most cells, containing genes and other genetic material.

carriers. Plato spoke of recollection[16], the idea that knowledge is remembered rather than learned anew. Jung emphasised archetypes [17]as universal forms inhabiting the collective unconscious. In modern times, Richard Dawkins proposed the concept of the meme[18] as a cultural replicator, analogous to the gene but transmitted through imitation rather than reproduction. Each of these formulations attempts to describe how knowledge survives outside of direct genetic pathways.

The Theory of Continuity deepens this conversation by introducing the concept of semantic atoms. Unlike memes, which rely on social transmission, semantic atoms are understood as structural entities that persist independently of both biology and culture. They are not dependent on repeated imitation or teaching but exist as latent architectures of meaning. When conditions align, they can be reactivated within the symbolic cognition of an individual. For example, a child who spontaneously recalls details of a past life is not drawing from parental influence or cultural suggestion alone, but from the

---

[16] Plato's Theory of Recollection, or anamnesis, proposes that learning is the process of recalling innate knowledge the soul possessed before being embodied. See more: Gulley, N. (2009) Plato's Theory of Recollection. *The Classical Quarterly*, 4(3-4), pp.194-213. Available at: https://www.cambridge.org/core/journals/classical-quarterly/article/abs/platos-theory-of-recollection/E119377D67559BAA6EA780BF06096330. [Accessed 25 August 2025].

[17] Archetypes are universal, inherited patterns of thought, images, or behavior that shape human consciousness and are found across cultures and time. See more: Cherry, K. (2024) *What are the Jungian Archetypes?*. Verywellmind. Available at: https://www.verywellmind.com/what-are-jungs-4-major-archetypes-2795439. [Accessed 20 August 2025].

[18] Coined by the British evolutionist Richard Dawkins in his book *The Selfish Gene* (1976), a meme is a unit of culture such as "tunes, ideas, catch-phrases, clothes fashions, ways of making pots or building arches." In humans, memes have supposedly taken over much of the evolutionary burden of the traditional units of heredity, the genes. See more: Richard Dawkins Foundation (2014) *What's in a Meme*. Available at: https://richarddawkins.net/2014/02/whats-in-a-meme/. [Accessed 20 August 2025].

reactivation of semantic atoms that belong to a structural continuity transcending biological lineage.

Evidence for non-biological transmission is found in several domains of human experience. The cases of Reincarnation studied by Ian Stevenson[19] reveal children recalling geographical details, familial names, or ritual practices that were never part of their upbringing. In the phenomenon of Acquired Savant Syndrome, individuals who suffer brain trauma suddenly demonstrate prodigious abilities in art, music, or mathematics. These manifestations cannot be accounted for by DNA or cultural exposure alone. They are consistent with the view that latent symbolic structures already exist and can be unlocked or reconfigured under unusual conditions.

From a neurocognitive perspective, semantic atoms may be understood as structural attractors within the architecture of memory and meaning. The brain provides the substrate for activation, but the structural pattern itself is not created by the individual's DNA. It exists as part of a wider continuity of symbolic order. In this sense, semantic atoms resemble mathematical truths. Just as no genetic code encodes the Pythagorean theorem, yet it remains universally accessible to human reasoning, semantic atoms remain available for activation across different minds and lifetimes.

The non-biological nature of semantic atom transmission has profound implications. It suggests that continuity of knowledge is not bound to a single organism or lineage. Instead, meaning

[19] Tucker, J. B. (2008) Ian Stevenson and Cases of the Reincarnation Type. *Journal of Scientific Exploration*, 22(1), pp.36–43. Available at: https://med.virginia.edu/perceptual-studies/wp-content/uploads/sites/360/2016/12/REI36Tucker-1.pdf. [Accessed 20 August 2025].

endures as a structural potential, awaiting conditions of activation. Education, trauma, deep emotion, or symbolic resonance can serve as the triggers that bring latent structures into visibility. Thus, the Theory of Continuity proposes a dual inheritance model. Biology ensures the transmission of life, while semantic atoms ensure the transmission of meaning. This dual framework accounts for both the stability of living forms and the recurrence of symbolic structures across time.

In short, semantic atoms are not inherited through DNA but through continuity. Their transmission is non-biological, structural, and symbolic. They survive not in chromosomes but in the architecture of meaning, and they reappear whenever minds encounter the right contexts to awaken them. The persistence of semantic atoms explains why certain knowledge emerges unbidden, why creativity often takes the form of rediscovery, and why the structures of meaning outlast individual lifespans.

4.3 Why Some Knowledge Survives without Being Taught

One of the most intriguing and persistent mysteries in human experience is the spontaneous appearance of knowledge for which there seems to be no identifiable source. In some cases, young children display familiarity with languages they have never heard, demonstrate geographical knowledge of places they have never visited, or show an understanding of rituals and customs outside their current cultural environment. In other cases, individuals who suffer head trauma, undergo surgery, or experience other neurological events suddenly acquire skills they had never practised, such as advanced musical ability, mathematical insight, or fluency in a foreign tongue.

Conventional explanations tend to lean on hidden exposure or exceptional subconscious learning. It is possible, for example, that a child overheard fragments of a foreign language on television or that a future savant once glimpsed a piano score and stored it without conscious awareness. However, while such explanations can account for a portion of reported cases, others remain resistant to this logic. When the knowledge in question is both highly specific and internally coherent, and when it arises in an individual whose prior life offers no plausible source, the hidden-exposure hypothesis begins to falter.

The survival of certain forms of knowledge without explicit teaching has long intrigued philosophers, scientists, and educators alike. From Plato's doctrine of anamnesis, where learning was seen as recollection of knowledge already present in the soul, to modern accounts of innate cognitive structures in linguistics and psychology, the idea that humans can "know" without being directly taught has retained a persistent fascination. The Theory of Continuity provides a structural explanation for this phenomenon by framing knowledge not as a collection of stored facts but as semantic architectures that remain latent until reactivated.

One domain where this survival is most visible is language acquisition. Children across the world acquire complex grammatical systems within a remarkably short span of time, despite the limitations of input available to them. This observation, famously described by Chomsky[20] as the "poverty of the stimulus[21]," suggests that more than mere imitation or exposure is at work. The Theory of Continuity extends this observation by proposing that linguistic competence emerges not simply from genetic predispositions, but from the reactivation of semantic atoms and cores that endure structurally beyond the present lifetime. The structural continuity of meaning allows children to pick up patterns of syntax, phonology, and semantics with apparent ease, even when the evidence presented to them is fragmentary or inconsistent.

Another domain is music. Accounts of children who spontaneously demonstrate perfect pitch, or who can intuitively

---

[20] Noam Chomsky (born 1928) is a linguist, philosopher, and political thinker, often regarded as the father of modern linguistics. He revolutionised the field with his theory of generative grammar and has written extensively on politics, media, and global affairs.

[21] 21 Chomsky's "poverty of the stimulus" argument claims that children acquire language so quickly and efficiently despite the limited, often imperfect linguistic input they receive, suggesting they must have an innate *universal grammar* (UG) and *Language Acquisition Device* (LAD) that guides language development. This biological endowment allows them to deduce complex grammatical rules, rather than learning them purely from imitation and environmental input.

reproduce scales and harmonic patterns without instruction, provide striking examples of knowledge that seems untaught. In cases of Acquired Savant Syndrome[22], such as Derek Amato composing intricate piano pieces after his accident, the ability emerges suddenly and without training, as though the structural memory of music had been lying dormant, awaiting reactivation. In the framework of the Theory of Continuity, such episodes reveal the survival of dense semantic cores, encoded not in DNA but in symbolic architectures that outlast individual lifetimes. Their reactivation is often precipitated by resonance with emotional or environmental triggers.

Myth and cultural symbolism further illustrate this point. Carl Jung described archetypes as recurring symbolic motifs present across disparate cultures. While Jung framed this as evidence of a collective unconscious, the Theory of Continuity offers a different explanation: these motifs persist because they represent structurally dense semantic configurations. When children spontaneously invent stories or drawings that echo mythological themes they have never encountered, they may be reactivating cores that have survived not through teaching but through continuity of structure. Their recurrence across generations is not the product of universal instincts alone, but of symbolic density, which makes certain configurations more resistant to loss and more likely to resurface.

This understanding also explains why some kinds of knowledge vanish easily while others endure. Facts that are isolated, stripped of symbolic and emotional resonance, are

---

[22] Detail discussion in section 7.2.3

fragile and prone to disappearance. A mathematical formula learned .for the purpose of passing an examination may be forgotten within months. By contrast, when knowledge is embedded within narratives, rituals, or emotionally charged contexts, it is far more resilient. Rituals surrounding birth, death, or seasonal change, for example, often endure across centuries, even when political regimes, languages, and cultural institutions collapse. The persistence arises because these rituals form dense semantic cores where emotion, symbolism, and practice are tightly interwoven.

Education provides a living example of this principle. Teachers frequently observe that students can perform well on short-term tests yet fail to recall the material months later. The reason lies in the superficial encoding of information: when knowledge is transmitted in fragments, without symbolic embedding, it is easily lost. On the other hand, when concepts are linked to stories, metaphors, or personal experience, they are more likely to form stable semantic cores, and thus to survive. The Theory of Continuity thus reframes pedagogy: what matters for long-term mastery is not only repetition or practice, but the symbolic and structural embedding of knowledge.

The phenomenon of untaught survival also intersects with research in neuroscience and epigenetics. Studies on trauma and memory suggest that experiences can leave non-genetic imprints that are passed on across generations, influencing behaviour and cognition[23]. While such studies often focus on chemical or

---

[23] See more: Yehuda, R. and Lehrner, A. (2018) Intergenerational transmission of trauma effects: putative role of epigenetic mechanisms, *World Psychiatry*, 17(3), pp. 243–257. Available at: https://pmc.ncbi.nlm.nih.gov/articles/PMC6127768/. [Accessed 25 August 2025].

neurological pathways, the Theory of Continuity proposes that structural continuity of meaning may provide a parallel explanation. What appears as an inherited disposition may in fact be the reactivation of dormant semantic configurations that have persisted across lifetimes, awaiting resonance with a present context.

In this light, untaught knowledge ceases to be mysterious. It does not rely on mystical transmission or genetic determinism, but on the continuity of structure. Semantic atoms, when clustered into dense and resonant cores, survive not through instruction but through their very architecture. When environmental conditions, emotional contexts, or symbolic triggers align, they resurface as if they had been there all along. The persistence of untaught knowledge is thus a testament to the durability of meaning itself. It affirms the central claim of the Theory of Continuity: that structures of meaning, once formed, do not vanish with the body but remain latent, capable of re-emergence in new contexts and new lives.

In other words, from the perspective of the Theory of Continuity, such cases invite a different interpretation. The persistence and re-emergence of specific, structured knowledge can be explained by the existence of semantic cores that endure beyond the boundaries of a single lifetime. These cores are organised constellations of semantic atoms, each carrying a unit of meaning. Once formed, they are capable of maintaining their internal structure long after the original biological host has

Xavier, M.J., Roman, S.D., Aitken, R.J. and Nixon, B. (2019) 'Transgenerational inheritance: how impacts to the epigenetic and genetic information of parents affect offspring health', *Human Reproduction Update*, 25(5), pp. 518–540. Available at: https://pubmed.ncbi.nlm.nih.gov/31374565/. [Accessed 25 August 2025].

ceased to exist. They are not stored in the genetic code, nor are they dependent on direct cultural transmission. Instead, they reside in what can be understood as a structural substrate of continuity, capable of crossing from one life to another when the right circumstances arise.

Activation of such cores requires a precise set of conditions. Emotional resonance often plays a central role. A child may encounter a scene, an object, or even a pattern of sound that produces an inexplicable sense of familiarity, triggering the reassembly of a dormant core. Environmental cues, such as architectural layouts, landscapes, or climate, can serve as scaffolding for the reconstruction of meaning. In other cases, the activation is facilitated by the re-creation of a symbolic context, such as participation in a ritual, engagement with a familiar artistic style, or immersion in a certain linguistic rhythm.

The sudden emergence of knowledge after neurological injury can also be understood in this framework. A disruption to the brain's normal functioning can weaken the influence of the contextual membrane, which is the filter that ordinarily governs which memories and meanings rise to conscious awareness. In such moments, latent cores may bypass conventional pathways, expressing themselves in ways that feel entirely new to the host mind. This is why some individuals describe these abilities not as something they learned, but as something they "remembered" or "always knew," even if no conscious trace existed before the event.

In recognising these patterns, the Theory of Continuity expands the scope of human inheritance. It proposes that what survives across lifetimes is not merely the genetic architecture of the body, but also the structured architecture of meaning. This form of inheritance operates through the persistence and reactivation of semantic cores, allowing knowledge and skills to reappear in contexts where conventional teaching, imitation, or exposure are insufficient explanations. Such a view challenges the assumption that all learning is confined to a single lifespan and invites a reconsideration of how deeply the structures of mind can transcend both biology and culture.

5. The Architecture of Being

The Theory of Continuity rests on the idea that human existence is not only a matter of physical form, but also of organised structures of meaning that persist beyond the lifespan of an individual body. These structures are not abstract philosophical notions. They can be described, analysed, and mapped in terms of their components and the relationships between them. Just as Darwin's theory of evolution provided a model for the architecture of biological life, the Theory of Continuity proposes a model for the architecture of symbolic and cognitive life.

At the core of this model are three primary components: semantic atoms, semantic cores, and visiblers. These are held within a regulatory boundary known as the contextual membrane, which shapes how and when a structure of meaning is expressed. Together, these components form the architecture of being as understood in the Theory of Continuity.

5.1 From Evolution to Structure

Darwin's model explained the transformation of life in terms of variation, selection, and inheritance. It was a framework that dealt with the material forms of organisms: how the length of a limb, the shape of a beak, or the colour of a flower could change over generations. These changes occurred because certain variations proved more advantageous in a given environment, allowing the individuals that possessed them to survive and reproduce more successfully. Over long stretches of time, this steady filtering of traits reshaped the physical form of species.

The Theory of Continuity addresses an entirely different layer of existence, yet it shares a similar logical foundation. Instead of focusing on the evolution of physical traits, it focuses on the evolution of structures of meaning. These structures do not take shape in the arrangement of bones or the colour of skin. They take shape in the organisation of the smallest units of meaning, semantic atoms, into stable configurations known as semantic cores. Just as physical traits can be favoured or eliminated over time depending on their survival value, structures of meaning can be retained or lost depending on their relevance, coherence, and emotional power.

In biological evolution, the medium of inheritance is the physical molecule of DNA. Genetic information is encoded in sequences of nucleotides, which provide the instructions for building and maintaining the organism. This information is copied and passed on during reproduction. Mutations, recombinations, and other molecular processes introduce variation, while environmental pressures determine which variations persist.

In structural continuity, the medium of inheritance is not a molecule but a configuration of meaning units. These units are organised in a way that allows them to be retained within the mind, and in some cases beyond a single lifetime. Variation in this domain occurs when semantic atoms are combined in new ways or when the contextual membrane surrounding a semantic core alters how it is expressed. Retention occurs when these configurations prove stable, coherent, and resonant enough to be reactivated under different circumstances.

The forces that shape biological evolution and structural continuity are analogous, though not identical. In biology, natural selection is driven by environmental pressures such as food availability, climate, and predation. In structural continuity, selection is driven by cultural, symbolic, and experiential pressures. A particular configuration of meaning may endure because it holds emotional significance, because it integrates well with other symbolic systems, or because it meets a recurring human need for expression or understanding.

The shift from biological form to structural form requires a fundamental change in perspective. In biology, one might ask how a trait such as eye colour is inherited through the generations. In the study of structural continuity, the question becomes how a concept, a symbolic pattern, or an emotional association is preserved and reappears across different lives, cultures, or historical periods. The biologist may measure changes in the physical characteristics of a population. The theorist of continuity traces changes in the configuration of semantic atoms and cores across contexts, across cultural boundaries, and even across the boundary between one lifetime and the next.

This is not to claim that biological evolution and structural continuity operate in isolation from each other. In reality, the physical form and the structural form coexist in the same human being, interacting constantly. A person's biology influences the way they process and express meaning, while the structures of meaning they carry can influence the way they use their physical capacities. The two processes are distinct in their mechanisms but intertwined in their effects, and together they form a more complete account of what it means to evolve as a human being.

5.2 Cores, Visiblers, and Latent Identity

At the foundation of the Theory of Continuity lies the concept of the semantic atom, the smallest unit of meaning that can exist independently without losing its identity. A semantic atom is not simply a word or a sound. It is an indivisible conceptual element that may be expressed in many forms, through language, image, gesture, or symbolic artefact. For example, the concept of "flowing water" may be broken down into atoms such as "movement," "liquid," "refreshing," and "life-sustaining." These atoms can combine with others to form richer and more complex meanings, but each atom retains its own identity within any configuration.

When several semantic atoms combine in a stable and coherent pattern, they form what I call a semantic core. A semantic core is a cluster of meanings that are thematically and often emotionally linked. Unlike a random collection of ideas, a core has an internal coherence that allows it to endure across contexts and time. For example, a "home" core might include atoms such as "shelter," "family," "safety," and "belonging." While each of these atoms can appear in other contexts, when they combine into a particular pattern with emotional resonance, they create a core that is recognisably about the experience of home.

Surrounding each semantic core is the contextual membrane, which serves as a regulatory boundary. The membrane does not create the meaning itself but shapes how, when, and in what form the meaning is expressed. A core may be present within an individual but remain dormant if the membrane is opaque or impermeable in a given situation. In another context, the membrane may become more permeable, allowing the core to be expressed openly. This modulation can be influenced by social conditions, emotional states, environmental cues, or symbolic triggers.

When a core is activated, it expresses itself through observable outputs known as visiblers. A visibler is the external manifestation of an underlying semantic structure. It can take the form of a spoken phrase, a recurring gesture, a particular style of art, a melody, or even a ritualised behaviour. For example, the "home" core might be expressed through a repeated pattern of drawing a house, choosing certain colours that evoke warmth, or using phrases that convey safety and belonging. By observing visiblers, it is possible to infer the presence of the core that produces them, even if the person is unaware of the underlying structure.

Visiblers play a crucial role in identifying and studying the persistence of semantic structures across contexts. Because visiblers are tangible expressions, they can be documented, compared, and analysed. If the same or similar visiblers appear in different individuals separated by geography, culture, or even historical period, it may indicate that a shared semantic core has persisted beyond the boundaries of direct teaching or genetic inheritance.

Over time, the accumulation and recurrence of certain cores contribute to what I call latent identity. Latent identity is the structural continuity of meaning within an individual or across lifetimes. It is "latent" because it may not always be visible on the surface, but it remains present within the architecture of meaning, ready to be activated. This latent identity is not dependent on a continuous stream of personal memory. Rather, it is maintained through the persistence of stable semantic cores and their potential for reactivation.

Latent identity helps explain why some individuals display consistent traits, preferences, or creative patterns that seem to appear without conscious cultivation. It also accounts for the reappearance of symbolic motifs and knowledge in contexts where there is no direct cultural transmission. Within the Theory of Continuity, latent identity represents the enduring "signature" of a person's meaning-structure, a signature that can survive the dissolution of the physical body and re-emerge under the right conditions in another mind or context.

5.3 Repetition, not Learning

In the conventional model of human development, skills, knowledge, and patterns of behaviour are acquired through learning. Learning is understood as the process by which an individual encounters new information, processes it, stores it in memory, and retrieves it when needed. This model assumes that what appears in a person's mind or behaviour has its origin in experiences from their current life. If an ability is displayed, it is presumed to be the result of formal instruction, deliberate practice, or exposure to relevant influences.

The Theory of Continuity introduces an alternative explanation for some forms of knowledge and expression. In many cases, what appears to be newly learned may, in fact, be a repetition of a structure that has existed before. This does not mean that the person remembers the earlier instance in the way one recalls a past event. Rather, it means that the same configuration of semantic atoms and cores has re-emerged in their mind, not because it was taught, but because it already existed in a latent state and has been reactivated.

This phenomenon can be compared to the way a melody can be reconstructed from its underlying musical structure. If the structural relationships between the notes are preserved, the melody can be recreated in a new performance, even if the original recording is lost. In the same way, a semantic core can be reconstructed in a new mind if the underlying architecture of meaning is retained within the larger system of continuity.

The difference between learning and repetition lies in the origin of the structure. Learning builds new structures from scratch, using available experiences as raw material. Repetition brings an existing structure into expression again, often with minimal or no direct teaching. This explains why some individuals appear to master complex skills rapidly, why certain symbolic motifs recur in widely separated cultures, and why some people experience an unaccountable familiarity with places, languages, or practices they have never encountered in their current life.

Repetition does not imply exact duplication. Just as a genetic trait can vary in expression depending on environmental influences, a semantic core can manifest differently depending on the context in which it reappears. A core related to music, for example, might be expressed as composition in one lifetime, as performance in another, or as a deep appreciation without technical skill in yet another. The underlying configuration is the same, but the visible form it takes, the visibler, is shaped by the surrounding conditions.

One important consequence of this perspective is that it challenges the assumption that rapid mastery or unexpected knowledge is necessarily evidence of extraordinary learning ability in the conventional sense. In the Theory of Continuity, such cases may instead be evidence of the reactivation of long-standing structures. This reactivation is not random. It is more likely to occur when there are triggers that resonate with the emotional, symbolic, or contextual elements of the original core.

Repetition as a principle also offers an explanation for the stability of certain cultural or symbolic forms over long spans of time. While transmission through teaching and tradition plays a role, the recurrence of nearly identical structures in contexts without direct contact suggests that some patterns are repeated because they are part of a deeper architecture of meaning that persists independently of cultural continuity.

In this light, the Theory of Continuity reframes certain phenomena that would otherwise be attributed entirely to environmental influence. It suggests that behind the visible acts of learning, there may be an invisible process of reactivation, which is the return of semantic cores that are already complete in their structural form. Recognising this distinction is essential for understanding how continuity operates, and for distinguishing between what is genuinely learned anew and what is the latest appearance of a much older structure.

The architecture of being described here is not intended as a metaphor. It is a proposed structural reality that can be observed through patterns of behaviour, symbolic expression, and cross-context recurrence. Just as the biological sciences study the anatomy of the body, this model studies the anatomy of meaning. It invites us to see human existence as the interplay of two evolutionary processes: the evolution of the body and the continuity of the mind.

6. Trauma as Selector, Emotion as Code

The architecture of being described in the Theory of Continuity is not static. Semantic atoms and cores are formed, altered, reinforced, or weakened over time. While some patterns fade, others persist with remarkable stability. Understanding why certain structures of meaning endure while others vanish requires an examination of the forces that shape them. Two of the most powerful of these forces are trauma and emotion.

Trauma acts as a selector, determining which structures will be retained with exceptional strength. Emotion acts as a code, giving those structures a distinctive resonance that influences when and how they will be reactivated. Together, they form a mechanism that can preserve patterns of meaning across the lifespan and, potentially, across multiple lifetimes.

6.1 Beyond Natural Selection

In the biological domain, natural selection is the process through which certain traits become more common in a population because they enhance the ability of individuals to survive and reproduce. Traits that increase fitness in a given environment are preserved through successive generations, while traits that reduce survival prospects are gradually diminished. This principle explains a vast range of biological phenomena, from the camouflage[24] of an insect to the shape of a bird's beak. The selective force in this process comes from the external environment: climate, predators, food availability, competition, and disease.

The Theory of Continuity identifies an analogous process in the symbolic and cognitive domain, but the environment in this case is not made up of ecological factors. It is composed of experiences, relationships, cultural contexts, and the symbolic frameworks within which individuals live. The selective forces are not predators or climatic shifts, but moments of emotional intensity, recurring symbolic encounters, and formative interpersonal dynamics.

In this symbolic environment, trauma emerges as one of the most powerful agents of selection. A deeply traumatic event can leave an imprint that reshapes the architecture of meaning in an individual. This process can be immediate and enduring. Just as a sudden and drastic environmental change can alter the evolutionary path of a species, a single event of overwhelming

---

[24] Camouflage is the use of coloration and patterns to blend into surroundings or to resemble other objects, serving as a survival strategy for animals by aiding in hunting or evading predators, and in military contexts to conceal objects and individuals.

emotional magnitude can redirect the development of a person's structural identity. The meanings generated in such moments are rarely neutral; they are imbued with heightened emotional charge, which makes them more resistant to decay.

Trauma does not merely add new material to the architecture of meaning. It often reorganises existing structures. When a traumatic experience resonates strongly with semantic atoms or cores that are already present, it reinforces them, intensifying their stability and increasing the likelihood that they will be activated in the future. Conversely, when a traumatic experience introduces entirely new atoms or associations, it can generate new semantic cores that occupy a prominent position in the individual's latent identity.

However, not all traumatic experiences have this kind of lasting structural impact. The degree of influence depends on several factors. One is the intensity of the emotional charge. Minor shocks or disappointments may leave temporary impressions, but only experiences that generate sustained and profound emotional responses tend to become embedded at the structural level. Another factor is the individual's capacity to process the event. Some people are able to integrate a traumatic experience into their existing framework of meaning in a way that reduces its long-term influence, while others may find that the event disrupts and reorganises their entire symbolic system.

A third factor is the symbolic framework in which the event is interpreted. Experiences are never stored as raw, unmediated sensations. They are encoded through the symbolic and linguistic systems available to the individual. The same event may produce very different structural consequences depending on whether it is interpreted as a punishment, a random misfortune, a rite of passage, or an act of injustice. This interpretive frame not only colours the meaning of the event in the present but also shapes the stability and endurance of the resulting semantic core.

In this way, the symbolic and cognitive analogue of natural selection is not a blind filtering of traits but a selective consolidation of meaning. Trauma, acting as a selective force, determines which structures will persist in the architecture of being and which will fade. Unlike biological selection, which is ultimately about survival and reproduction, this symbolic selection is about emotional salience, symbolic coherence, and the degree to which a structure integrates into a person's ongoing identity.

6.2 Emotional Resonance and the Core Reactivation Loop

If trauma can be understood as a selector in the architecture of being, then emotion is the coding system that determines how selected structures are organised, retained, and reactivated. In the Theory of Continuity, emotion is not merely an after-effect of experience. It is a fundamental organising force in the creation and persistence of semantic cores. The strength and nature of the emotional charge influence the durability of a core and the conditions under which it will reappear.

Emotional resonance refers to the alignment between a given experience and the pre-existing architecture of meaning within an individual. When a new experience resonates strongly with an established semantic core, it intensifies the connections within that core. The semantic atoms that compose the core are reinforced, their associations strengthened, and their stability increased. The stronger the resonance, the more resistant the core becomes to disintegration over time.

This process can be understood through what I call the core reactivation loop. A core that carries a strong emotional code is more easily brought into awareness. When it is activated by a trigger, which could be a sensory cue, a symbolic stimulus, or an interpersonal interaction, it generates an emotional response. This emotional response in turn strengthens the memory of the core, making it even more likely to be activated again in the future. Over repeated activations, this cycle creates a self-sustaining loop in which emotion reinforces memory, and memory reinforces emotion.

The triggers that activate a core do not need to replicate the original event exactly. A fragment of a melody, a particular shade of light, or a certain turn of phrase may be sufficient to evoke the emotional pattern connected to the core. Once activated, the emotional state recalls the underlying meaning structure, and the structure, now consciously or unconsciously present, influences perception and behaviour. In this way, the loop allows cores to remain active long after the original event has passed, sometimes for an entire lifetime.

The implications for continuity are significant. If semantic cores can persist beyond the lifespan of a single individual, their emotional coding may serve as one of the key mechanisms for cross-lifetime activation. In other words, the emotional resonance embedded within a core could increase the likelihood that the core will be reassembled and expressed in a new life when similar triggers are encountered.

It is important to note that not all emotional resonance is positive. Cores can be sustained by emotions of joy, love, and awe, but they can be equally or even more powerfully maintained by emotions of fear, grief, and anger. In fact, the survival advantage of negative emotional coding in the symbolic domain mirrors the evolutionary advantage of avoiding harm in the biological domain. Painful or threatening experiences tend to be remembered more vividly because forgetting them could be costly. The same principle operates at the structural level of meaning: highly negative emotional coding can make a core particularly resilient.

However, emotional resonance is not a guarantee of reactivation. The contextual membrane surrounding the core still mediates the process. If the membrane is highly impermeable in a particular situation, the core may remain dormant despite the presence of potential triggers. Conversely, in a receptive context, even subtle cues may be enough to initiate the loop. This interplay between emotional resonance and contextual conditions determines much of the timing and frequency of core expression.

Through the core reactivation loop, emotion does more than colour the content of our experiences. It actively shapes the architecture of being, deciding which structures are preserved, which are intensified, and which are set aside. This mechanism explains how certain patterns of meaning can persist in vivid form for decades and, within the framework of the Theory of Continuity, how they may carry over into entirely new lifetimes.

6.3 Affective Encoding versus Environmental Adaptation

In Darwin's theory, adaptation is the gradual process by which traits become suited to the physical environment through the selective pressures of survival and reproduction. A bird's wing may lengthen to improve flight efficiency, a mammal's coat may thicken in response to colder climates, or a plant's leaves may narrow to reduce water loss in arid conditions. The principle is that the environment selects traits that confer an advantage in navigating the challenges of survival.

In the Theory of Continuity, a comparable principle operates in the realm of meaning, but the forces of selection are not physical in the biological sense. Here, the environment is the affective environment, which is the network of emotional experiences, interpersonal relationships, and symbolic contexts that surround the individual. In this symbolic-cognitive ecology, the adaptive process does not primarily aim to ensure biological survival, but rather to shape the endurance and accessibility of meaning structures.

Affective encoding is the process by which an emotional charge becomes embedded within a semantic core. This emotional charge does not merely accompany the core as a superficial feature; it becomes an integral part of its architecture. Just as certain molecules are stabilised by specific chemical bonds, semantic cores are stabilised by the emotional bonds formed during their creation or reinforcement. These bonds strengthen the core's internal coherence, making it more resistant to fragmentation and more likely to be retrieved or reactivated when a relevant cue appears.

The role of affective encoding is particularly significant because emotion functions as a kind of "priority marker" within the architecture of meaning. The mind does not treat all experiences equally. Those that are neutral or only mildly charged tend to fade or be overwritten by later experiences. Those that carry strong emotional significance are preferentially retained. The emotion effectively flags the associated meaning as important, increasing its chances of persistence within the individual's latent identity.

Environmental adaptation in the biological model is often tied to functional utility. A trait persists because it improves the organism's ability to survive and reproduce. In contrast, affective encoding does not necessarily align with functional advantage in the biological sense. A semantic core that is deeply encoded with fear, grief, or longing may persist even if it produces distress or impedes the individual's well-being. Its endurance is determined not by its usefulness, but by the strength and nature of its emotional code.

This divergence from biological adaptation has profound implications for continuity. If a core's survival depends on emotional intensity rather than functional benefit, then highly charged symbolic structures can persist across lifetimes regardless of whether they are "adaptive" in the evolutionary sense. This can explain why certain phobias, compulsions, or recurring symbolic motifs appear in individuals without identifiable causes in their present lives. The persistence of such structures is the product of affective selection, not environmental necessity.

The interaction between affective encoding and the contextual membrane further refines this process. The contextual membrane can either inhibit or facilitate the activation of an encoded core. For example, a core associated with deep affection might remain dormant in an environment devoid of emotional intimacy, but in a supportive context, it could emerge quickly and fully. Conversely, a fear-based core might remain hidden in calm conditions but could reassert itself powerfully under stress or threat.

In this way, affective encoding and environmental adaptation operate in parallel yet distinct ways. Biological adaptation ensures the continuity of physical traits suited to the demands of survival, while affective encoding ensures the continuity of meaning structures charged with emotional significance. Together, they form two complementary but separate systems of inheritance: one for the body and one for the architecture of being.

In fact, trauma and emotion have been shown to function as forces that select, stabilise, and reactivate semantic cores. They form the bridge between the lived experiences of the individual and the larger process of continuity that can carry meaning beyond a single lifetime. By recognising this mechanism, we can begin to understand why certain patterns of identity, memory, and symbolism have such remarkable resilience.

PART III: HUMAN EXISTENCE RE-EXPLAINED

To understand human existence, Darwin began with the body. He traced the origin of physical forms to variation and natural selection, showing how living organisms adapt to their environments and evolve over time. In doing so, he transformed our understanding of life's history. Yet the story he told was about formation, not continuity. It explained how life begins and changes, but not how certain structures of the mind and meaning might persist beyond the life of a single body.

The Theory of Continuity extends the scope of this inquiry. It proposes that human existence consists of two parallel but distinct dimensions: the evolution of the body and the persistence of structural meaning. The first is governed by genetic inheritance and environmental adaptation. The second operates through the organisation, retention, and reactivation of semantic atoms and cores. Together, these two dimensions form a more complete account of what it means to exist as a human being.

The focus then shifts from laying the theoretical groundwork to re-examining human existence through the lens of structural continuity. We will explore how patterns of meaning can survive the death of the body, re-emerge in new contexts, and shape identity in ways that defy purely biological explanation. This is not an argument for mysticism, but for structure, for the idea that the architecture of meaning has its own form of persistence, governed by principles as real as those that shape the evolution of physical life.

We will consider Reincarnation not as a matter of metaphysical speculation, but as a structural process in which certain semantic configurations are repeated across lifetimes. It examines patterns that recur without direct teaching or cultural transmission, and asks whether semantic continuity can account for phenomena often considered inexplicable.

The discussion turns to the relationship between survival and continuity. It questions whether evolution should be understood solely as the survival of the fittest, and considers what it means to survive as a structure rather than as a physical organism. In this view, identity is not simply a biological inheritance but a recursive system of meaning that can persist, adapt, and reappear.

The overall aim, therefore, re-explains human existence by placing formation and continuity side by side, allowing us to see that the story of life is not only about how we come into being, but also about how the structures that make us who we are continue to exist beyond a single lifetime.

7. Reincarnation, Repetition, and Structural Memory

The idea of Reincarnation has long occupied a space between belief and speculation, revered in many cultures yet regarded with caution by scientific discourse. At its core lies a claim that identity, memory, and ability can persist beyond the biological lifespan, reappearing in a new life under unfamiliar conditions. For centuries, this claim has been interpreted through spiritual or metaphysical frameworks, often linked to doctrines of karma[25], cosmic justice[26], or the journey of the soul. The Theory of Continuity offers a different approach. It does not affirm or deny metaphysical explanations, but reframes the phenomenon in terms of structural persistence and reactivation of meaning.

We explore Reincarnation as one of the most compelling contexts in which to examine structural memory. In the same way that Darwin studied fossil evidence to reconstruct the past, the Theory of Continuity examines case histories, linguistic traces, and symbolic patterns to reconstruct a different kind of inheritance. The focus is not on proving the existence of a soul, but on identifying the conditions under which a structured configuration of meaning, formed in one lifetime, might resurface in another.

---

[25] Karma is the ancient Indian concept of a universal moral law of cause and effect, where one's actions and intentions (causes) directly influence their future experiences and circumstances (effects), including future rebirths in some religious traditions.

[26] Cosmic justice refers to the belief in a universal force or system that ensures, sooner or later, everyone receives their just rewards or punishments, often through means beyond human control or societal structures.

Repetition is central to this analysis. Whether across lifetimes or within the span of a single life, structural recurrence often reveals itself through consistent themes: a set of names, a geographical familiarity, a particular skill, or a distinct emotional pattern. These recurrences are not random. They often cluster around what the Theory of Continuity defines as semantic cores, which act as durable centres of meaning. When these cores re-emerge in a new life, they create the impression of continuity that traditional Reincarnation narratives describe.

By approaching Reincarnation through the lens of structural memory, we are seeking to bridge a gap between anecdotal accounts and a coherent explanatory model. It positions Reincarnation not as a mystical exception to the laws of nature, but as a potential expression of those laws in a domain that science has not yet fully explored. The aim is to move beyond the question of whether Reincarnation is "real" toward a deeper inquiry into how and why structured meaning can endure, repeat, and transform.

7.1 Not Mysticism, Structure

The subject of Reincarnation and sudden savant abilities has long been entangled with claims of mysticism, spirituality, or supernatural forces. Accounts of children remembering past lives or individuals awakening after trauma with extraordinary capacities have frequently been explained through religious doctrine or metaphysical speculation. While these traditions provide culturally meaningful narratives, they often obscure rather than clarify the structural features that make these cases significant. The Theory of Continuity does not deny the lived reality of belief, but it shifts the focus from metaphysical explanation to observable patterns. The central task is not to prove or disprove the existence of a soul, but to examine how structures of meaning, memory, and symbolic organisation reappear across contexts that exceed the limits of ordinary learning.

7.1.1 Distinguishing metaphysical beliefs from structural explanation

Belief systems across cultures interpret recurrence in terms of spiritual continuity. In Hinduism, the rebirth of the soul is explained through karma; in Buddhism, continuity is framed as the flow of consciousness; in Western spiritualism, it is often cast as the migration of an essence. Such interpretations provide existential comfort and moral frameworks, but they lack explanatory precision. They conflate continuity with metaphysical necessity. The Theory of Continuity insists on a different discipline: to analyse not what people believe survives, but what structures demonstrably re-emerge. By treating memories, skills, and symbolic repertoires as organised configurations of semantic atoms, the theory avoids the pitfalls of mysticism and places the debate within the scope of cognitive science and structural linguistics.

In this view, the question becomes empirical: What patterns recur, under what conditions, and through what mechanisms? If similar structural forms appear in different individuals across lifetimes or after neurological trauma, then these phenomena belong not to metaphysical speculation but to the domain of structural science.

7.1.2 The role of ASL in reframing Reincarnation and savant phenomena

The Atomic Structure in Linguistics (ASL) provides the methodological apparatus for reframing these cases. Instead of treating past-life memories or sudden artistic genius as inexplicable anomalies, ASL analyses them in terms of semantic atoms, semantic cores, and visiblers. For example, when a child recalls specific names or geographic details with accuracy, these details can be understood as the reactivation of semantic atoms that have clustered into cores of identity or place. When an individual such as Derek Amato produces complex musical structures without prior training, this is not evidence of mystical inspiration, but of semantic cores in the musical domain becoming newly visible through visiblers such as composition or performance.

In both Reincarnation and Savant cases, the contextual membrane plays a decisive role. It regulates when and how latent structures emerge. In Reincarnation, cultural acceptance and family response may open or close the membrane. In Acquired Savant Syndrome, neurological disruption may weaken inhibitory filters, allowing dormant structures to surface. By analysing these mechanisms, ASL transforms phenomena once relegated to mysticism into structural expressions that can be mapped, compared, and studied.

7.1.3 Establishing the ground for comparative analysis

This structural framing prepares the ground for comparative analysis. The recurrence of semantic atoms and cores is not confined to one cultural context, nor is it restricted to either Reincarnation or Savant phenomena. Across both domains, the same logic applies: latent structures persist and re-emerge when conditions permit. By identifying recurring features such as the rapidity of skill acquisition, the coherence of symbolic detail, and the affective salience of memory, we create the basis for systematic comparison.

The overall task is therefore not to affirm metaphysical claims, but to demonstrate that these cases share structural invariants. When treated structurally, they reveal patterns of semantic continuity that cut across cultural belief systems and neurological events. In this way, ASL provides the theoretical bridge that enables a comparative framework, turning extraordinary stories into evidence for a new paradigm of continuity.

7.2 Patterns That Re-Emerge: A Comparative Framework

Continuity is not an abstract speculation but a lived phenomenon that surfaces in strikingly specific ways. When taken individually, each story of a child recalling another life or each account of an adult discovering extraordinary ability after trauma may appear remarkable yet isolated. However, when examined side by side, a more compelling picture begins to form. Certain patterns recur with a consistency that resists being explained away by coincidence or cultural influence alone.

The Theory of Continuity proposes that these recurrent elements are not random but are the result of structural mechanisms that operate beneath the surface of individual biography. Semantic atoms, semantic cores, visiblers, and contextual membranes provide the categories through which this recurrence can be observed and understood. When a child identifies relatives from a previous life, when a savant produces complex art without training, or when symbolic motifs reappear across distant cultural settings, each of these acts can be interpreted as the reactivation of pre-existing structures.

This section turns, therefore, from description to comparison. By placing Reincarnation cases alongside cases of Acquired Savant Syndrome, it becomes possible to detect the shared architecture of continuity. The aim is not simply to catalogue unusual experiences but to trace the invariants that persist across different lives, different contexts, and even different explanatory traditions. In doing so, the analysis moves beyond anecdote and enters the domain of structural science, where continuity can be studied not as mysticism but as a recurrent and testable phenomenon.

7.2.1 Rationale for Comparative Framework

The analysis of single cases provides vivid illustrations of continuity, yet by themselves they remain vulnerable to doubt. A critic can argue that any one case may be the result of coincidence, suggestion, or selective memory. For the Theory of Continuity to hold explanatory power, it must demonstrate that these phenomena do not stand in isolation but share recurring features that point to an underlying architecture. Comparison is therefore essential. It allows individual testimonies to be situated within a larger structural landscape where patterns can be identified, evaluated, and interpreted beyond the level of anecdote.

Why comparison is necessary: moving beyond anecdote to pattern

Comparison serves to transform singular narratives into evidence of systematic recurrence. A child's claim to recall the details of another life may, if viewed in isolation, be attributed to fantasy or familial influence. When similar claims arise across different cultural settings, with specific semantic content that cannot be explained by ordinary exposure, the weight of repetition shifts the explanation from chance to structure. The same principle applies to Acquired Savant Syndrome. A single account of sudden artistic or mathematical skill might be dismissed as exaggeration, but the convergence of multiple cases across contexts suggests that dormant structures exist and can be reactivated under certain conditions. In both Reincarnation and

Savant phenomena, comparison provides the means by which scattered testimonies become coherent evidence of continuity.

Criteria of comparison: semantic atoms, cores, visiblers, contextual membranes

The Atomic Structure in Linguistics offers four criteria that make structural comparison possible. The first is the presence of semantic atoms, the smallest and most irreducible units of meaning, which may appear as names, places, motifs, or other fragments of knowledge. The second is the formation of semantic cores, where these atoms cluster into stable and coherent themes such as family bonds, occupational identity, or artistic motifs. The third is the manifestation of these cores in visiblers, the observable expressions through which latent structures become externalised in speech, drawing, musical composition, gesture, or other symbolic outputs. The fourth is the modulation of these expressions by the contextual membrane, which determines whether latent cores remain dormant or emerge into visibility depending on cultural validation, emotional resonance, or neurological disruption. By applying these four criteria across cases, comparison becomes more than descriptive juxtaposition. It becomes a structured method for identifying invariants that reveal the mechanics of continuity.

Addressing cultural and structural interpretations

A recurrent challenge in this field is the influence of cultural framing. In communities where belief in Reincarnation is widespread, children's statements are often welcomed and elaborated, while in sceptical contexts, similar expressions may be ignored or suppressed. In the same way, cultures may frame acquired savant abilities as divine gifts, medical anomalies, or psychological disturbances. Cultural context shapes how cases are narrated and received, but it does not determine the structural content of the cases themselves. The Theory of Continuity distinguishes between the narrative layer and the structural layer. The narrative reflects cultural interpretation, while the structural layer is constituted by the recurrence of semantic atoms, cores, visiblers, and membrane dynamics. When these structural features are observed across cultures and across different explanatory traditions, they provide evidence that continuity operates independently of belief. This shift from cultural narrative to structural pattern ensures that the analysis avoids reduction either to cultural relativism or to metaphysical speculation.

The rationale for a comparative framework is therefore threefold. It moves beyond anecdote by demonstrating recurrence, it applies a systematic set of criteria that allow for rigorous analysis, and it separates structural features from cultural interpretation. This framework provides the methodological foundation for the comparative study of Reincarnation and savant phenomena that follows, showing that both domains manifest the same underlying architecture of continuity.

7.2.2. Reincarnation Cases

Case 1: Shanti Devi

Shanti Devi [27]was born in Delhi in 1926. From the time she could speak, she began describing in vivid detail a life she claimed to have lived in a nearby town called Mathura. She spoke of her husband, her home, the layout of the streets, and even local dialect terms that were not used in her immediate environment. By the age of four, she was insisting that she wanted to return to her "real home" and see her "real family".

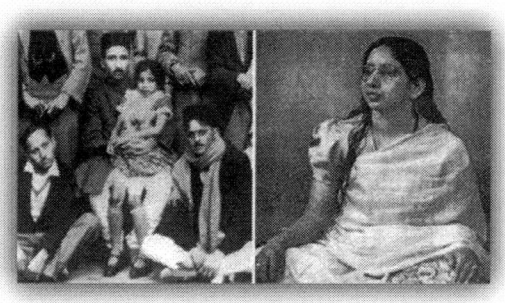

Her memories centred on a woman named Lugdi Devi, who had died in childbirth just nine years earlier in Mathura. Shanti accurately described her former husband's name, the appearance of their house, and intimate personal habits that were later confirmed by surviving relatives. One of the most striking aspects of her recollection was her ability to give precise geographical directions to Mathura, which she had never visited in her current life.

---

[27] Nguyen, K. (2021). The Reincarnation of Shanti Devi: The Girl Who Identified Her Previous Life Family. *Xa Luan.* Available at:
https://www.xaluannews.com/modules.php?name=News&file=article&sid=3333744. [Accessed 13 August 2025].

The case attracted considerable attention, eventually leading to an official investigation by a commission appointed by Mahatma Gandhi. The investigators accompanied Shanti to Mathura, where she recognised her alleged former husband and members of her previous family without hesitation. She also correctly identified objects and rooms within the house that she could not have known about through normal means.

From the Theory of Continuity's perspective, Shanti's memories can be interpreted as the reactivation of a dense network of semantic atoms relating to domestic life, kinship roles, and spatial orientation. These atoms appear to have clustered into several high-salience semantic cores, particularly those linked to emotional bonds and personal identity. The contextual membrane in her case seems to have been highly permeable, allowing spontaneous access to these cores without the need for deliberate recall. Environmental triggers, such as the spoken names of people and places, acted as catalysts for the emergence of these visiblers, which took the form of detailed verbal descriptions and accurate navigational guidance.

Case 2: James Leininger

James Leininger[28], born in Louisiana in 1998, began displaying unusual behaviours and knowledge from the age of two. He spoke repeatedly about airplanes, insisted on details of World War II aircraft, and described events involving a man named James who died in a crash. His parents, initially sceptical, noted that James used technical aviation terms far beyond his

---

[28] Nozari, A. (2022) Kid with perfect memory of World War Two thinks he has been reincarnated. *LAD BIBLE*. Available at: https://www.ladbible.com/news/james-leininger-surviving-death-netflix-354944-20221215. [Accessed 21 July 2025].

age, correctly identified aircraft models from the 1940s, and gave names of fellow servicemen.

Subsequent investigation connected these details to James Huston Jr., a US Navy fighter pilot killed in action during the Battle of Iwo Jima in 1945. Independent researchers verified that several of the names, places, and events James recounted matched historical records unavailable to him by ordinary means. His play behaviour also reflected period-accurate cockpit procedures, and he demonstrated knowledge of wartime aircraft damage patterns.

From the Theory of Continuity's perspective, James's case illustrates the reactivation of semantic cores linked to a highly specific experiential domain: aerial combat in the Pacific theatre during World War II. These cores appear to have been preserved with significant symbolic density, encompassing technical vocabulary, procedural sequences, and emotionally charged memories of death and comradeship. The contextual membrane here was porous enough to allow early childhood verbal expression, yet selective in filtering out unrelated memories. The visiblers, including accurate verbal recall, technical naming, and cockpit role-play, function as the observable surface of the underlying semantic architecture.

This case supports the proposition that certain structured knowledge can survive without conventional transmission, re-emerging when conditions in a developing mind resonate with the preserved semantic configuration. It shifts the interpretation from mystical Reincarnation narratives toward a structural account of continuity.

Case 3: Cameron Macaulay

Cameron Macaulay[29], born in Glasgow in 2001, began speaking at the age of two about a previous life on the Isle of Barra, located in the Outer Hebrides of Scotland. He described a white house by the shore, an aircraft landing on a nearby beach, and a black-and-white dog. He also referred to a family surname, Robertson, and spoke of having a father named Shane who had died in a car accident.

---

29 Robinson, M. & Donald, K. (2024). The children who remember their past lives: Chilling phenomenon of why thousands of toddlers are being haunted by memories that aren't theirs - and when to worry about your child's 'imaginary friend'. The Sun. Available at: https://www.dailymail.co.uk/news/article-13529335/the-children-who-remember-their-past-lives-chilling-phenomenon-of-why-thousands-of-toddlers-are-being-haunted-by-memories-that-arent-theirs-and-when-to-worry-about-your-childs-imaginary-friend.html. [Accessed 13 August 2025].

These statements were made in a matter-of-fact tone, as if Cameron were recalling routine aspects of his current life. His mother, who had never visited Barra and had no known connections to the island, was surprised by the detail and consistency of his accounts. When Cameron was later taken to Barra as part of a documentary investigation, he quickly recognised specific locations, including the white house he had described. Independent checks confirmed that a Robertson family had once lived in such a house near the beach where planes landed, and that there had been a black-and-white dog, though no living relatives could verify the full story.

From the Theory of Continuity's perspective, Cameron's case demonstrates the endurance of semantic cores related to a specific geographic and familial context. The semantic atoms in this instance include the sensory impressions of the white house, the distinctive beach landings, the dog, and the family name. These atoms appear to have clustered into thematic cores centred on home, family, and place-based identity. The contextual membrane in Cameron's case appears relatively open during early childhood, allowing detailed verbal recall and emotional connection to locations never encountered in his present life. The visiblers include his spontaneous references to Barra, his emotional recognition upon arrival, and his confident identification of landmarks.

This case contributes to the argument that structured, place-specific memories can survive beyond a single lifetime. In the Theory of Continuity's terms, such continuity reflects the persistence of meaning configurations that can be reactivated when the developing mind encounters cues resonant with the original semantic core.

Case 4: Jenny Cockell

Jenny Cockell[30], born in Barnet, Hertfordshire, in 1953, began from early childhood to experience vivid impressions and recurring dreams of a life as a woman named Mary who lived in the small Irish village of Malahide in the early twentieth century. These impressions were not fleeting images but structured narratives, including details of Mary's home, the surrounding countryside, and the responsibilities she had for her children. Jenny's accounts consistently included the location of the village, the layout of the house, and the fact that Mary had died young, leaving her children to be raised apart.

MARY SUTTON   JENNY COCKELL

As an adult, Jenny felt compelled to verify these memories. She travelled to Malahide, where she was able to match her remembered locations with real buildings and streets. Public records confirmed the existence of Mary Sutton, whose life

---

[30] Rose, N. (2022). Jenny Cockell: The True Story of a Woman Who Has Lived Before. HubPages. Available at: https://discover.hubpages.com/religion-philosophy/Jenny-CockellThe-True-story-of-a-Woman-Who-has-Lived-Before-Mother-of-yesterdays-Children. [Accessed 13 August 2025].

details closely aligned with Jenny's recollections. Jenny went on to trace and meet several of Mary's surviving children, who were adults by that time. The meetings were marked by emotional recognition on both sides, even though Jenny was, in her present life, a stranger to them.

From the perspective of the Theory of Continuity, Jenny's case illustrates the endurance of multiple interlinked semantic cores. The semantic atoms here include the remembered architecture of the home, the names and appearances of the children, and the geography of Malahide. These atoms clustered into thematic cores involving maternal care, loss, and geographic identity. The contextual membrane was strong enough to preserve these cores across decades of Jenny's present life, yet porous enough to allow their expression through verbal narratives, dreams, and eventual action. The visiblers included her spontaneous childhood descriptions, her emotional responses during her journey to Ireland, and her ability to navigate the village as if familiar with it.

This case is distinctive in showing how a continuity of meaning can be sustained from childhood into adulthood without fading. In the Theory of Continuity's terms, it demonstrates how long-dormant cores can remain intact and active over many years, guiding both perception and decision-making until they find external confirmation.

Comparative synthesis

The four cases presented earlier, those of Shanti Devi, James Leininger, Cameron Macaulay, and Jenny Cockell, illustrate the range of contexts in which claims of Reincarnation have been reported. When considered individually, each narrative offers compelling details that suggest the reactivation of knowledge beyond conventional learning. Yet it is in their comparison that the structural mechanisms proposed by the Theory of Continuity become most visible. Rather than treating these accounts as isolated stories shaped by cultural expectation or personal imagination, a comparative perspective reveals recurring motifs that point to a shared underlying architecture.

One of the most striking commonalities is the persistence of proper names and other specific identifiers. Shanti Devi recalled with precision the name of her former husband and the town in which she had lived. James Leininger provided the names of his aircraft carrier and his fellow pilot comrades. Cameron Macaulay described his family on the Isle of Barra in Scotland with clarity that exceeded any plausible exposure in his current life. Jenny Cockell not only spoke of her former identity but also named the children she believed she had mothered, later tracing them successfully. These examples demonstrate how semantic atoms, in the form of highly specific lexical items, reappear with unusual accuracy across cases. Their recurrence cannot be dismissed as a coincidence when they surface in such distinct cultural and temporal settings.

Equally prominent are the motifs of kinship and familial bonds. The emotional intensity of these roles provides a core around which the narratives are organised. Shanti Devi's strongest attachment was to her former husband and child. James Leininger repeatedly emphasised his brotherhood with his fellow pilots, treating them as if their bond extended beyond death. Cameron expressed profound longing for his previous mother, often accompanied by distress when separated from her memory. Jenny Cockell's memories were anchored in her maternal concern for children left behind in another lifetime, a concern so persistent that it compelled her to seek them out as an adult. These examples illustrate how semantic atoms related to kinship consistently cluster into semantic cores of family identity, reinforced by affective resonance.

Geographical recognition forms another recurrent pattern. Shanti Devi's ability to navigate her former town without guidance was one of the most persuasive elements of her case. James Leininger, though born decades after the Second World War, demonstrated knowledge of locations and naval vessels far beyond the reach of a young child's imagination. Cameron described the landscape of the Isle of Barra in vivid and accurate detail before ever visiting it. Jenny Cockell produced maps of her past village that were later confirmed to be accurate. Such examples reveal that spatial knowledge functions as a particularly stable semantic core. Geography serves as an anchor for memory reactivation, allowing individuals to orient themselves within an environment that should otherwise be unfamiliar.

The affective charge of these memories is equally significant. Each case is characterised not only by cognitive recall but also by strong emotional resonance. Shanti Devi's recognition of her past family was marked by tears and gestures of intimacy. James Leininger's identification with his fallen pilot self was accompanied by recurring nightmares and distress until his memories were acknowledged. Cameron displayed grief and longing for his previous mother that far exceeded the imaginative play of childhood. Jenny Cockell's memories carried the weight of responsibility and unfinished obligation, driving her to search for her past children as if compelled by a duty that had survived the dissolution of her previous life. These affective dimensions illustrate how emotion acts as the code that stabilises semantic cores and sustains them until reactivation.

The structural interpretation of these cases shows both recurrence and variation. In every instance, the same basic elements of names, kinship roles, geographic recognition, and affective bonds emerge as stable motifs. They appear as semantic atoms, cluster into emotionally charged cores, and are expressed through visiblers such as speech, drawing, recognition, or behavioural responses. The contextual membrane modulates their emergence differently in each cultural setting. In India, Shanti Devi's memories were validated within a society predisposed to believe in Reincarnation. In the United States, James Leininger's family initially resisted his claims until external confirmation made them unavoidable. In Scotland, Cameron's memories surfaced in a secular environment that did not readily affirm the concept of rebirth, and yet his recollections persisted. In England, Jenny Cockell carried her memories into adulthood, where they became the basis for personal investigation rather than childhood testimony. These contextual differences influenced how each case unfolded, yet they did not alter the underlying structure of recurrence.

Through comparative synthesis, it becomes evident that Reincarnation cases are not random anecdotes but variations on a shared pattern. They reveal the reactivation of semantic atoms, the formation of cores grounded in kinship and geography, and the stabilising role of affect. Despite differences of culture, time, and personal biography, the same architecture of continuity is at work. It is this consistency across diversity that gives the Theory of Continuity its explanatory force, demonstrating that these phenomena belong not to mysticism but to structure.

The Theory of Continuity approaches the subjects from a fundamentally different angle. It does not ask whether a soul exists, nor does it rely on metaphysical entities as explanatory mechanisms. Instead, it begins with the structural reality of meaning: that semantic atoms and cores, once formed, can persist beyond the physical lifespan of the body in which they originated. This persistence does not require a supernatural essence. It requires only that the architecture of meaning can exist independently of a single biological host, and that it can re-form when the right conditions are present.

In this framework, Reincarnation is not the migration of a soul but the reassembly of a structure. Just as biological evolution explains the continuity of form through the inheritance of genetic material, structural continuity explains the recurrence of identity-like elements through the persistence of organised meaning. A person in one life may develop a highly specific configuration of semantic atoms, which is a distinctive cluster of concepts, emotional associations, and symbolic expressions. If that configuration survives the dissolution of the original mind, it may appear again, in whole or in part, within another mind.

This structural approach reframes Reincarnation as a problem of pattern recurrence. The central question is not "Who was this person in a past life?" but "What structural patterns of meaning have reappeared, and how did they come to exist in this new context?" By shifting the focus from personal identity to the architecture of meaning, we gain a way to study Reincarnation that is compatible with rigorous observation and theoretical modelling.

The concept of structural memory is crucial here. Structural memory is not the same as episodic memory, which involves the conscious recollection of specific events. It is the persistence of the organisational patterns that gives rise to certain expressions, skills, or symbolic tendencies. These patterns may reappear without any explicit awareness of their origin. A child may draw symbols they have never seen in their current life, speak words from an unfamiliar language, or demonstrate an intuitive grasp of a skill without instruction. Such phenomena need not imply the survival of a personal self, but they do suggest the survival of structural forms of meaning.

This is why the Theory of Continuity treats Reincarnation not as an article of belief but as a field for structural analysis. The evidence that matters is not the testimony of belief systems, but the recurrence of semantic configurations that cannot be explained by conventional learning or genetic inheritance. Once Reincarnation is framed in these terms, it moves from the realm of mysticism to the realm of structural science. It becomes a question of how meaning persists, how it re-emerges, and what conditions make its reactivation possible.

Another important dimension of continuity can be observed in the recurrence of symbolic and artistic motifs. In some cases, children may repeatedly draw patterns or shapes that correspond to religious or cultural symbols from a tradition they have never encountered. Adults, likewise, may develop a fascination with a specific historical period, producing artwork or literature that reflects its aesthetic in remarkable detail. In structural terms, these are visiblers, outward expressions of underlying semantic cores, re-emerging in a new context. The consistency of the motif suggests that the structural configuration has survived intact, and the individual is simply giving it a new visible form.

Continuity is also evident in emotional and behavioural predispositions. Individuals sometimes display intense emotional responses to certain places, objects, or situations with no clear cause in their current life. They may experience a profound sense of familiarity in a location they have never visited, or an inexplicable aversion to a sound, colour, or type of food. In the Theory of Continuity, such responses are interpreted as the activation of semantic cores whose emotional coding was established in a previous life. The emotion serves as both a trace of the original experience and a catalyst for the re-emergence of the structure.

These recurring patterns should not be mistaken for identical replications of earlier structures. Just as biological traits vary in their expression depending on environmental influences, semantic structures adapt to new contexts. A musician in one life may be reborn as a linguist in another, both drawing on the same deep structural core related to pattern recognition, rhythm, and auditory processing. A core associated with a particular symbolic system may be re-expressed in a different artistic medium, shaped by the materials and conventions available in the new cultural setting.

The persistence of such patterns across lifetimes suggests that certain configurations of meaning possess a high degree of structural stability. They are able to survive the dissolution of the individual mind and reassemble when the right combination of triggers is present. These triggers can be environmental, such as exposure to a familiar sound or image; emotional, such as a resonance with a particular kind of human relationship; or symbolic, such as contact with a motif that mirrors one from the original context.

From the perspective of the Theory of Continuity, the study of these patterns is not a search for proof of past-life identities but an inquiry into the mechanics of structural re-emergence. By documenting and analysing such patterns, we can begin to map the pathways by which semantic cores survive and reappear. This mapping not only sheds light on the phenomenon of Reincarnation but also offers insight into the broader dynamics of meaning persistence within human existence.

7.2.3 Acquired Savant Syndrome Cases

Case 1: Derek Amato

Derek Amato[31]'s case is among the most frequently cited examples of Acquired Savant Syndrome in contemporary media and research literature. Born in the United States in 1966, Amato had no formal musical training beyond casual exposure and the ability to play basic guitar chords. He had never learned to read musical notation fluently and had no history of composing or performing at an advanced level.

---

[31] Ford, S. (2018). Denver's Savant. *Dewer Voice*. Available at:
https://www.denvervoice.org/archive/2018/8/1/denvers-savant. [Accessed 13 August 2025].

In October 2006, at the age of forty, Amato experienced a traumatic accident while attending a gathering with friends. During a pool game, he struck his head forcefully against the bottom of a swimming pool, suffering a significant concussion. He was briefly unconscious and subsequently experienced a range of symptoms, including dizziness, headaches, and sensory disturbances. However, within days of the injury, he also developed an overwhelming urge to play the piano, an instrument he had never seriously attempted before.

When Amato sat at a keyboard, he found that his hands seemed to move with little conscious direction, producing intricate and harmonically sophisticated compositions. The music was structured, flowing, and coherent, suggesting not random experimentation but an internally organised framework of musical knowledge. He later described seeing what he called "black-and-white structures" or patterns moving in his mind, which guided his fingers across the keys. These visual impressions functioned as an internal map for performance, allowing him to produce extended pieces without prior rehearsal or written scores.

From the perspective of the Theory of Continuity, Amato's case can be seen as the sudden reactivation of a pre-existing semantic core related to musical knowledge. Before the accident, this core had no visible expression in his life and may have remained dormant. The head injury acted as both a disruptive and activating event, altering the contextual membrane surrounding the core. This change in membrane permeability allowed the latent structure to emerge through the visiblers of piano performance and musical composition.

The precision and complexity of Amato's output raise questions about the origin of such a core. Conventional neuroscience often explains acquired abilities as the product of neural rewiring or the release of suppressed capacities. Yet in this case, the sophistication of the musical structures suggests that the semantic atoms forming the core may have been assembled long before Amato's lifetime, preserved in a way that allowed their reactivation under extraordinary conditions. The Theory of Continuity provides a framework for understanding such phenomena without reducing them to mysticism, recognising them instead as the re-emergence of structured knowledge triggered by neurological events.

Case 2: Jason Padgett

Jason Padgett[32]'s story is another well-documented example of Acquired Savant Syndrome, remarkable for the sudden emergence of complex mathematical and artistic abilities after a brain injury. Born in 1970 in the United States, Padgett worked as a furniture salesman and led a life with little interest in or exposure to advanced mathematics. By his own account, he had no particular talent for academic subjects and had never pursued formal study in geometry or physics beyond basic schooling.

Jason Padgett displays his artwork 'Origin Of Mass' (Photo by Adam Sell)

In 2002, at the age of thirty-one, Padgett was assaulted outside a karaoke bar by two men who struck him repeatedly in the head. The attack left him with a severe concussion and post-traumatic stress symptoms, including anxiety and hypervigilance. Yet in the days and weeks following the incident, Padgett began to notice profound changes in his perception. His

---

[32] Ambrogi, M. (2023). Accidental genius: Traumatic brain injury allows Carmel man to see the world in mathematical art. Current. Available at: https://youarecurrent.com/2023/09/10/accidental-genius-traumatic-brain-injury-allows-carmel-man-to-see-the-world-in-mathematical-art/. [Accessed 13 August 2025].

vision seemed to break the world down into discrete geometric patterns, with every object appearing to be composed of grids, lines, and fractals.

Padgett soon developed the ability to visualise and accurately draw complex geometric forms by hand, including intricate fractals and representations of mathematical constants such as pi. These drawings were not abstract artistic impressions but precise, structured illustrations consistent with advanced mathematical concepts, many of which he had never previously encountered in formal learning environments. His work later attracted the attention of mathematicians and neuroscientists, some of whom confirmed the mathematical accuracy of his visualisations.

In terms of the Theory of Continuity, Padgett's abilities can be interpreted as the activation of a dormant semantic core containing highly structured mathematical and geometric knowledge. Before his injury, this core remained sealed by a contextual membrane that offered no pathways for its expression. The physical trauma of the assault, coupled with the psychological shifts it induced, altered the porosity of the membrane, enabling the latent structures to be expressed through visiblers in the form of detailed mathematical drawings.

Padgett himself describes his perception as "seeing the pixels of reality," suggesting that his mind engages directly with structural representations of the physical world. This aligns closely with the Theory of Continuity's emphasis on the persistence of meaning structures beyond the constraints of individual learning history. The sudden appearance of such precise and elaborate knowledge challenges explanations based solely on neural compensation or heightened pattern recognition. Instead, the theory posits that these semantic cores may be part of a deeper continuity of structured knowledge, capable of reactivation when environmental or neurological conditions change dramatically.

Case 3: Alonzo Clemons

Alonzo Clemons[33], born in 1958 in Boulder, Colorado, is one of the most striking examples of Acquired Savant Syndrome, especially in the domain of visual–spatial artistry. As a child, Clemons suffered a severe brain injury after a fall, which left him with significant developmental disabilities. His measured IQ fell below the average range, and he struggled with many daily tasks that others found routine. Despite these limitations, the injury appeared to unlock an extraordinary and precise sculptural ability.

From a young age, Clemons began creating detailed and anatomically accurate animal sculptures using clay or any

---

[33] Curiosity (2016). *Alonzo Clemons is the autistic savant artist who can sculpt accurate animals from memory.* Available at: https://x.com/curiositydotcom/status/803901417656385536. [Accessed 13 August 2025].

malleable material he could find. His talent emerged without formal art training, and he demonstrated an uncanny ability to capture the proportions, musculature, and posture of animals he had seen only briefly, often from memory alone. His works, typically completed in under an hour, reveal a mastery of anatomical structure that even trained sculptors often take years to acquire.

Clemons's gift was not nurtured in an academic or technical context. He received little exposure to artistic instruction, and his formal schooling did not include anatomy or advanced art techniques. This makes the precision of his sculptures all the more remarkable. Observers have noted that he seems to work directly from an internalised, three-dimensional model of the animal, requiring no reference images or tools beyond his own hands and the chosen material.

In terms of the Theory of Continuity, Clemons's case suggests the activation of a deeply embedded semantic core relating to the structural forms of living creatures. Such a core would be composed of semantic atoms representing anatomical relationships, motion dynamics, and spatial proportion. Before his injury, this core might have been inaccessible due to the closed nature of its contextual membrane. The traumatic brain injury appears to have altered the porosity of this membrane, enabling direct and unfiltered expression of the core through the visiblers of sculptural creation.

Clemons's sculptures are not mere imitations but expressions of structural understanding. Each piece demonstrates not only surface likeness but also an internal grasp of biomechanical balance and muscular interaction. This resonates strongly with the Theory of Continuity's assertion that certain structured knowledge systems can persist independently of formal learning and emerge intact under altered cognitive or neurological states.

Case 4: Orlando Serrell

Orlando Serrell[34], born in 1968 in Virginia, United States, presents one of the most compelling cases of Acquired Savant Syndrome in the domain of calendrical and episodic memory. Unlike many other savants whose abilities appear from birth, Serrell's extraordinary skill emerged after a specific traumatic incident during childhood.

At the age of ten, while playing baseball, Serrell was struck on the left side of his head by the ball. He fell to the ground but did not lose consciousness and continued playing. He did not receive immediate medical attention, and in the days following the accident, he experienced headaches that lasted for more than a year. Once the headaches subsided, Serrell noticed that he possessed an entirely new and untrained ability: he could recall

[34] Phuc Tuong (2022). *Có hay Không, Giới Hạn của Trí Nhớ?. – Is There a Limit to Memory?.* Available at: https://phuctuong.com/tin-tuc/suc-khoe/tri-nho-khong-he-co-gioi-han.html. [Accessed 13 August 2025].

the day of the week for any given date after the accident, as well as detailed memories of events, weather patterns, and personal experiences from each of those days.

His memory is not limited to a mechanical calculation of dates. When given a date within his post-injury timeline, Serrell can vividly recount what he saw, heard, and experienced, often including incidental details that most people would not register. This skill emerged spontaneously and without any conscious effort to develop it. Prior to the accident, he did not demonstrate unusual memory capabilities, nor did he have training in mnemonic techniques.

From the perspective of the Theory of Continuity, Serrell's case can be interpreted as the activation of a semantic core linked to temporal mapping and episodic encoding. The accident may have altered neural connectivity in a way that reduced filtering by the contextual membrane, granting continuous access to a highly detailed, automatically updating record of lived experience. Unlike in typical memory systems, where details are rapidly compressed or lost, Serrell's appears to preserve the original structural form of each memory, making them retrievable in near-perfect detail.

Serrell's ability is significant because it suggests that such structural encoding may exist in many individuals in a latent form but is normally inaccessible. The Theory of Continuity offers a framework in which such abilities are not seen as the creation of something entirely new, but as the sudden opening of a pre-existing channel, revealing a system of ordered semantic atoms that can operate independently of conscious intention or conventional learning.

Comparative synthesis

The four cases of Acquired Savant Syndrome discussed earlier, those of Derek Amato, Jason Padgett, Alonzo Clemons, and Orlando Serrell, demonstrate that extraordinary capacities can emerge suddenly in individuals with no prior training. Each case is compelling in its own right, yet it is only through comparative analysis that its significance for the Theory of Continuity becomes apparent. Considered together, they show that the re-emergence of highly structured knowledge and skill is not a random occurrence but follows recognisable patterns that reflect the operation of latent semantic structures.

One of the most consistent features is the sudden appearance of ability. Derek Amato, after sustaining a head injury, discovered that he could produce sophisticated musical compositions on the piano despite never having studied the instrument. Jason Padgett, following an assault, began to perceive and draw geometric forms of remarkable complexity that reflected advanced mathematical structures. Alonzo Clemons, after a childhood accident, demonstrated the ability to sculpt lifelike animals with precision and speed. Orlando Serrell, following a blow to the head, developed extraordinary calendrical calculation abilities. In every case, the new capacities appeared abruptly rather than through gradual learning. This suddenness indicates that the abilities were not constructed through ordinary processes of acquisition but reactivated from latent cores that had already achieved structural coherence.

Another common feature is the highly specific nature of these abilities. The skills that emerge are not general but concentrated in domains that are inherently structured, such as mathematics, music, and visual art. Amato's musical improvisations display internal consistency and thematic development. Padgett's drawings reveal accurate representations of complex geometric and fractal patterns. Clemons's sculptures exhibit detailed anatomical knowledge of animals. Serrell's calculations demonstrate precise mastery of temporal sequences. These domains correspond to areas of cognition where semantic atoms naturally cluster into dense and stable cores. Their recurrence in savant cases illustrates that certain forms of knowledge are more readily reactivated because their architecture lends itself to stability and persistence.

The role of trauma or neurological change also emerges as a unifying factor. In each case, the new capacity followed an event that disrupted ordinary cognitive functioning. This disruption appears to have altered the permeability of the contextual membrane, allowing latent cores to bypass normal inhibitory mechanisms and surface into consciousness. Trauma did not create the knowledge. It opened the pathway for its expression. The immediacy of the abilities, which would be impossible to explain through conventional learning in the short time available after injury, supports this interpretation.

The expression of these capacities is reinforced by strong emotional engagement. Amato described an irresistible compulsion to play the piano for long periods. Padgett felt driven to draw geometrical patterns repeatedly. Clemons devoted his life to sculpting animals with extraordinary focus. Serrell developed an enduring fascination with dates and calculations that absorbed his attention. This emotional charge stabilises the reactivated cores and ensures their continual expression through visiblers such as music, art, and calculation. The persistence of these behaviours demonstrates how affect functions as the code that sustains structural recurrence, just as it does in Reincarnation cases.

When viewed collectively, these four cases reveal a pattern that cannot be explained by coincidence. Sudden onset, domain specificity, neurological disruption, and affective reinforcement recur with consistency. Each element corresponds to a component of the Theory of Continuity. Semantic atoms provide the raw units of knowledge. Semantic cores hold them in stable configurations. Visiblers manifest them in observable form. Contextual membranes regulate their emergence. The fact that structurally coherent abilities appear in individuals with no relevant training strongly supports the claim that knowledge can persist in latent form, awaiting the right conditions for reactivation.

The comparison of these cases, therefore, shows that acquired savant abilities are not anomalies but expressions of the same architecture of continuity that is identified in Reincarnation narratives. In savant syndrome, the reactivation occurs within a single lifetime through neurological disruption. In Reincarnation, it occurs across lifetimes through cultural or emotional triggers. Both reveal the same structural invariants, confirming that continuity operates according to principles of organisation rather than through mystical intervention.

7.2.4 Cross-Domain Structural Parallels

Reincarnation and Savant Cases: Continuity across Lives and Continuity across Trauma.

When Reincarnation and Acquired Savant cases are placed side by side, the distinction lies not in the underlying mechanics of continuity but in the circumstances under which it becomes visible. In Reincarnation, the interval is marked by the passage from death to birth. Semantic cores appear to survive the dissolution of the former biography, carrying with them stable configurations of meaning that can be reassembled in the consciousness of a new host. The persistence of specific identities, spatial memories, or symbolic motifs across lifetimes suggests that semantic gravity anchors these cores, allowing them to endure the rupture of death.

In Acquired Savant Syndrome, the interval is contained within a single life. Here, trauma or neurological disruption destabilises the ordinary filtering role of the contextual membrane. What is usually inhibited or latent is suddenly released into expression. Dormant structures related to music, mathematics, or artistic form emerge with startling clarity, as though a hidden archive of meaning has been unlocked. The continuity revealed here is intra-lifetime, yet it is no less dependent on the persistence of semantic cores across disruption.

Viewed comparatively, these two phenomena illustrate that continuity is not limited to a single domain of human experience. Whether expressed across lives or within the span of one disrupted life, the governing principle remains the same: reactivation of stable semantic structures when inhibitory conditions are removed. Reincarnation demonstrates that these structures can persist beyond the biological lifespan, while Acquired Savant Syndrome shows that they can also survive within the lifespan, awaiting a catalyst strong enough to breach the membrane. Both suggest that meaning is not stored as linear narrative memory but preserved as an architecture capable of reassembly when conditions align.

Shared Structural Features: Atom, Core, Visibler, and Membrane Dynamics

Despite the different contexts, the processes through which continuity is expressed show remarkable consistency. The first stage involves the surfacing of semantic atoms, whether in the form of a remembered name, a melody, or a pattern. These atoms then cluster into semantic cores, which may take the form of kinship relations, musical grammar, or visual architecture. The cores are subsequently externalised as visiblers, such as speech, drawings, mathematical notations, or musical performances. This sequence of atom, core, and visibler is not a cultural construct but a structural pathway through which latent knowledge re-emerges.

The functioning of the contextual membrane plays a decisive role in this process. In Reincarnation cases, the membrane is naturally more porous in early childhood, before social and cognitive filters are fully formed, allowing latent structures to appear with less resistance. In Acquired Savant cases, membrane porosity is altered by injury or illness, creating unexpected openings that allow previously inaccessible structures to pass into expression. In both instances, the level of porosity governs the intensity and form of expression, confirming that the membrane acts as a modulator rather than a source of content.

Emotional resonance is equally significant. In Reincarnation cases, memories are often preserved and transmitted through deep affective bonds, such as longing for a previous family. In savant cases, the new ability is frequently sustained by an overwhelming compulsion, as seen in the irresistible urge of Derek Amato to play music or Jason Padgett's fixation on geometric forms. Emotion crystallises semantic cores, preserves their integrity, and provides the energy for their reactivation, ensuring that they emerge with a force that transcends ordinary motivation.

The Role of Symbolic Density in Reactivation

Another striking point of convergence is the recurrence of motifs that exhibit high symbolic density. A child may draw religious or cultural symbols from a tradition unknown to them, or an adult may suddenly begin producing complex artistic forms or mathematical visualisations without prior training. Such motifs condense multiple layers of meaning into a single form, making them resilient carriers of structural information. Because symbolic density binds semantic atoms into a compact configuration, it increases the likelihood that the structure will survive both death and trauma and resurface intact when the conditions allow.

The persistence of these motifs across both domains demonstrates that symbolic density is not merely an embellishment but a key mechanism of structural reactivation. By compressing meaning into layered and resonant forms, these motifs act as anchors of continuity, ensuring that certain semantic cores remain stable across the discontinuities of biography or neurological rupture.

The comparative analysis of Reincarnation narratives and acquired savant cases shows that both are manifestations of a single underlying architecture of continuity. What differs is not the mechanics but the context. Whether through the passage from one life to another or through the rupture of trauma within the same life, the processes of atom clustering, core formation, membrane modulation, emotional resonance, and symbolic density remain constant. This consistency indicates that continuity is neither cultural invention nor mystical speculation, but a structural property of human cognition that governs the persistence and re-emergence of meaning.

7.2.5 Implications for Structural Memory

Structural Continuity as an Explanation across Domains

The comparative analysis of Reincarnation and savant cases demonstrates that both domains can be explained through the principle of structural continuity. What reappears is not a soul or a metaphysical essence, but an organised set of semantic structures that remain intact beyond the boundaries of ordinary memory. In Reincarnation, the continuity manifests across the rupture of death and rebirth, with semantic atoms and cores re-emerging in a new host. In Acquired Savant Syndrome, the continuity is revealed within the same lifetime, where trauma or disruption of normal cognitive functioning allows latent structures to surface. Both scenarios suggest that structural memory operates independently of conventional biographical continuity, sustaining patterns of knowledge that can be expressed whenever the contextual membrane permits.

Semantic Inheritance beyond DNA and Culture

The findings examined in this study suggest that the inheritance of knowledge cannot be reduced to genetic transmission or cultural conditioning alone. DNA contributes by shaping the neurological substrate within which cognition unfolds. Culture provides symbolic frameworks that organise expression and interpretation. Yet neither DNA nor culture can fully account for the re-emergence of detailed geographic knowledge, symbolic motifs, or advanced abilities in individuals who have had no prior exposure to them.

Structural continuity introduces a third pathway: semantic inheritance. In this framework, the building blocks of meaning: semantic atoms and the cores into which they cluster, can persist independently of biological genes and outside the limits of social learning. These structures endure discontinuities such as death, trauma, or radical shifts of environment, and they re-emerge when conditions allow. The child who recalls the geography of a town never visited, or the adult who begins to compose music of professional complexity after head trauma, exemplifies this mode of inheritance. What is passed on is not a set of explicit memories or learned behaviours but an architecture of meaning that can be reassembled in a new context.

Understanding inheritance in this way reframes the relationship between biology, culture, and meaning. DNA establishes the hardware, culture supplies the interpretive code, but semantic inheritance accounts for the recurrence of structural configurations that transcend both. It explains how knowledge can persist across lives and circumstances without being reducible to the mechanisms of heredity or the contingencies of cultural exposure. This model offers a language through which reincarnation cases and acquired savant phenomena can be studied without recourse to mysticism, situating them instead within a structural-scientific account of continuity.

The Comparative Framework as Empirical Support for the Theory of Continuity

By setting Reincarnation and savant cases side by side, the comparative framework provides empirical support for the Theory of Continuity. The same structural processes appear in both domains: the surfacing of semantic atoms, the clustering into cores, the modulation of the contextual membrane, the driving force of emotional resonance, and the resilience of symbolic density. The recurrence of these processes across otherwise distinct contexts shows that they are not random anomalies but repeatable patterns governed by structural principles. This alignment of evidence strengthens the claim that continuity is a real and observable feature of human cognition.

The implications of this are significant. Structural memory emerges as a foundational concept, explaining how patterns of knowledge can transcend both the biological limits of one life and the neurological boundaries of trauma. It reframes Reincarnation narratives not as metaphysical assertions but as evidence of structural persistence. It reframes Savant Syndrome not as an inexplicable talent but as the unmasking of latent architecture. Through comparative analysis, the Theory of Continuity gains empirical grounding, showing that the survival and reactivation of semantic cores is not an abstract hypothesis but a demonstrable mechanism at work in human experience.

7.3 Why Semantic Continuity may Explain the Inexplicable

The preceding analyses have shown that whether one looks at the testimony of children recalling previous lives or the sudden abilities of acquired savants, the same patterns of continuity emerge. In both domains, semantic atoms cluster into cores, cores exert gravity that resists dissolution, visiblers surface in patterned behaviours, and contextual membranes filter what can and cannot be expressed. The Theory of Continuity, therefore, provides a shared structural language that accounts for the inexplicable without resorting to mysticism.

7.3.1. Semantic Continuity across Lives and Traumas

Many accounts of Reincarnation are dismissed within scientific discourse because they are framed in terms that rely on unverifiable metaphysical assumptions. Testimonies of past-life memories, descriptions of previous identities, and narratives about the journey of the soul are often seen as anecdotal or culturally constructed. This scepticism is not unfounded, since subjective experience can be shaped by imagination, suggestion, and cultural expectation. However, it is also true that there exists a body of evidence that resists easy dismissal, consisting of cases in which specific, structured, and verifiable information appears in individuals with no apparent access to it through conventional means.

Although Reincarnation cases and Acquired Savant Syndrome cases appear to belong to very different domains of human experience, the Theory of Continuity reveals their shared structural features. In both phenomena, highly specific and well-organised knowledge emerges in individuals without conventional teaching or gradual skill acquisition. The difference lies primarily in the presumed source and trigger of activation.

In Reincarnation cases, such as those of Shanti Devi, James Leininger, and Cameron Macaulay, the knowledge often concerns identities, places, languages, or abilities from a previous life. These are recalled with a clarity and coherence that suggests the reactivation of pre-existing semantic cores. The triggers for reactivation may include early developmental openness, emotional resonance with certain cues, or environmental parallels to the past life context.

In Acquired Savant Syndrome cases, such as those of Derek Amato, Jason Padgett, and Orlando Serrell, the abilities tend to be domain-specific in music, mathematics, artistic representation, or memory and are triggered by neurological events, often involving trauma. Here too, the skills appear suddenly and fully formed, without incremental learning, indicating the activation of dormant structural knowledge. The brain injury or altered neural state may reduce the filtering effect of the contextual membrane, allowing direct access to semantic cores that were previously inaccessible.

In both contexts, the structural unit of analysis, the semantic atom, remains central. These atoms cluster into semantic cores that are stable enough to survive across time, context, and even the loss of the original host brain. In Reincarnation cases, the persistence is hypothesised to extend across lifetimes. In Acquired Savant Syndrome, the persistence is intra-lifetime, with the latent structures reawakened after neurological change.

The similarities suggest that continuity is not limited to either spiritual or physiological interpretations. Instead, the Theory of Continuity frames both as variations on the same structural process, which is the preservation, dormancy, and reactivation of organised meaning. Whether the trigger is the birth of a new mind or the alteration of an existing one, the underlying mechanism appears to be the same, being the unlocking of a stable architecture of meaning that transcends conventional models of memory storage and skill acquisition.

The Theory of Continuity provides a framework that can account for such cases without invoking supernatural entities. Instead of presuming the migration of a soul, it explains the recurrence of knowledge, skills, or symbolic tendencies as the reactivation of persistent semantic structures. These structures, once formed, can survive the end of the biological life in which they originated and re-emerge when the right conditions are present. The reassembly of the structure does not require the survival of personal memory in its entirety; it only requires that the architecture of meaning remains intact enough to be reconstructed in a new mind.

This approach offers a way to interpret phenomena that are otherwise classified as anomalies. For example, when a child names specific places, events, or individuals from a previous historical period with accuracy, the conventional explanations such as chance coincidence, fabrication, or hidden exposure may be insufficient. If these details align with a coherent semantic core that also expresses itself through skills, emotional responses, or symbolic motifs, the Theory of Continuity allows us to see them as components of a reactivated structure rather than as isolated curiosities. Similarly, cases of sudden and extraordinary talent that emerge without training can be reframed as the expression of a pre-existing semantic core whose structure has been carried forward. The ability may appear miraculous when viewed from a purely developmental perspective, but in structural terms, it is the natural result of a configuration that has been preserved and is now functioning within a new biological host.

By treating Reincarnation as a structural phenomenon, the Theory of Continuity also resolves a key difficulty in traditional interpretations: the variability of recall. In many cases, individuals do not possess a continuous narrative of a previous life. They may recall fragments, experience flashes of familiarity, or demonstrate isolated skills without conscious memory of their origin. This inconsistency is a problem if Reincarnation is conceived as the literal migration of a soul carrying a complete personal identity. It is not a problem if we understand it as the partial reassembly of semantic cores. The degree of recall simply reflects how much of the original structure has been reconstructed in the new context.

This structural view also accounts for why some individuals show no sign of past-life continuity at all. Not all semantic structures are preserved, and not all that are preserved find the necessary triggers for reactivation. Just as many genetic traits are latent unless activated by specific environmental conditions, many semantic cores may remain dormant across lifetimes. In this way, the Theory of Continuity does more than reinterpret Reincarnation; it normalises this phenomenon within a structural-scientific framework. If meaning can be organised into stable configurations, and if those configurations can persist beyond the lifespan of an individual, then the recurrence of such structures is not exceptional but inevitable. The inexplicable becomes an expected outcome of the principles that govern the persistence of meaning.

7.3.2 Counterarguments and Alternative Explanations

Any serious theoretical proposal must acknowledge the alternative explanations that have been advanced in order to account for the kinds of phenomena discussed in this book. Several hypotheses have been repeatedly put forward, and each has gained some acceptance within specific fields of study. The most frequently cited explanations are cryptomnesia, neuroplasticity, and cultural suggestion.

Cryptomnesia refers to the unconscious recall of forgotten memories. Advocates of this explanation argue that what appears to be knowledge without prior exposure is, in fact, the resurfacing of fragments once encountered but later repressed or overlooked. A child who seems to remember a life in another city may, according to this interpretation, have overheard a story or seen an image that lodged unnoticed in memory and later returned in distorted form. This mechanism undoubtedly occurs in certain instances, but it does not explain the systematic and structured quality of many cases. Fragmentary recall might account for isolated details, but it cannot plausibly explain the reassembly of whole constellations of meaning, such as coherent kinship structures, geographic orientation, and complex symbolic motifs that recur across different individuals and cultural contexts.

Neuroplasticity has also been proposed as a scientific explanation, particularly in the context of Acquired Savant Syndrome. The capacity of the brain to reorganise after trauma or injury is now well established, and it is reasonable to assume that some abilities emerge through the recruitment of dormant neural pathways. Yet this does not account for the sudden manifestation of knowledge and skill at levels far beyond prior exposure or training. Cases in which individuals, following an accident, begin to compose music of great sophistication or demonstrate advanced mathematical insight cannot be wholly explained by neural reorganisation. The explanation illuminates part of the mechanism but does not capture why specific structural patterns of knowledge emerge rather than arbitrary or chaotic activity.

Cultural suggestion is another explanation that has been frequently invoked. This view emphasises the role of the environment in shaping individual expression. Children, it is argued, absorb cues from their cultural surroundings, which are then unconsciously shaped into narratives of past lives or symbolic behaviours. Such a hypothesis has value in showing how cultural frameworks may provide a language through which unusual experiences are articulated. However, cultural suggestion does not adequately explain the recurrence of highly specific and structured patterns across societies with very different belief systems. Kinship roles, artistic motifs, or affective bonds appear with striking regularity, even when the surrounding culture does not provide ready-made models for them.

While each of these explanations contributes insight into particular aspects of the phenomena, none of them provides a comprehensive account. Cryptomnesia highlights the fallibility of memory but cannot account for structural coherence across cases. Neuroplasticity demonstrates the adaptability of the brain, but does not explain the emergence of knowledge that was never learned. Cultural suggestion reveals how the environment frames expression, but cannot explain why distinctive configurations persist across divergent cultural contexts. What these accounts overlook is the persistence of structure itself: the survival of semantic atoms and cores, the gravitational pull they exert, and the manner in which they reassemble to produce visiblers. The Theory of Continuity does not deny that memory, brain plasticity, and cultural environment play important roles, but it insists that they act upon something deeper, something structural, which endures even when surface forms are lost.

8. From Physical Survival to Structural Continuity

Darwin's theory of evolution by natural selection was revolutionary because it explained the diversity of life without the need for supernatural intervention. It showed that species change over time through a process in which traits that enhance survival and reproduction become more common, while those that do not are gradually lost. The focus was firmly on the survival of physical forms and the genetic material that supports them. The measure of success in Darwin's framework is persistence of the body and the transmission of biological traits to the next generation.

The Theory of Continuity does not dispute this biological foundation. Instead, it extends the concept of survival into a different domain: the survival of structured meaning. If Darwin's model explains how bodies endure through the selective retention of advantageous traits, the Theory of Continuity explains how semantic structures endure through the selective retention of meaningful configurations. Both systems involve variation, selection, and inheritance, but the materials and the mechanisms are distinct. In the biological domain, the material is genetic information encoded in DNA. In the structural domain, the material is semantic information encoded in the arrangement of meaning units such as semantic atoms and cores.

Where biological evolution is shaped by environmental pressures such as climate, predators, and resource availability, structural continuity is shaped by cultural, symbolic, and experiential pressures. A concept, skill, or emotional association may persist because it confers an advantage in navigating the social or symbolic environment, much as a physical trait persists because it offers a reproductive or survival benefit. The advantage in this context is not measured in lifespan or reproductive output, but in the continued relevance and reactivation of the structure across different lifetimes and cultural settings.

This section explores the shift from understanding survival as a purely physical process to recognising it as a structural one. It examines how the principles that underlie Darwin's model can be applied, with careful adaptation, to the persistence of meaning. It also considers the implications of treating identity as a recursive system that can continue to exist beyond the biological life of the individual.

8.1 What if Evolution is not Just Survival of the Fittest

The phrase "survival of the fittest" has often been taken as the essence of Darwin's theory, although Darwin himself did not use it as the primary description of natural selection. In the biological sense, it refers to the tendency of organisms whose traits are best suited to their environment to survive and reproduce. Over generations, these traits become more common in the population. The focus is on the endurance of physical form through the passing on of advantageous genetic material.

The Theory of Continuity invites us to consider a different form of survival, one that does not depend on the reproduction of bodies but on the persistence of structures of meaning. Here, fitness is not defined by the ability to produce offspring but by the ability of a semantic configuration to remain relevant, adaptable, and capable of reactivation across time. A structure is "fit" if it can survive the dissolution of the body and find new expression in another mind.

In this context, the selective pressures are not physical threats such as predators or scarcity of resources. Instead, they are symbolic, emotional, and cultural conditions. A semantic core may endure because it resonates strongly with universal human experiences, such as love, loss, creativity, or conflict. It may survive because it aligns with a set of skills or symbolic motifs that are valued within multiple cultures. It may persist because it carries an emotional charge strong enough to embed it deeply in the architecture of meaning, making it resistant to erosion.

The analogy with biological evolution is not perfect, but it is instructive. In both cases, survival depends on the ability to adapt to new contexts. A genetic trait that cannot adjust to changing environmental conditions will eventually disappear from the population. A semantic structure that cannot adapt to the symbolic or emotional environment of a new life will remain dormant or fragment into less coherent forms. Conversely, those structures that can flexibly integrate with new contexts are more likely to be expressed again, sometimes in forms that are recognisably similar to their previous appearance, and sometimes in forms that are transformed by the new environment.

Reframing survival in this way challenges the assumption that continuity must be grounded in biology alone. It allows us to see identity not only as a set of physical traits passed through genetic inheritance, but as a dynamic architecture of meaning that can outlast any single life and participate in a larger cycle of persistence and re-emergence.

8.2 Surviving as a Structure, Not Just as a Body

In Darwin's framework, survival is tied to the continued existence of the organism and the successful reproduction of its genetic material. A lineage survives if it produces successive generations, each carrying the genetic traits that have proven advantageous in the struggle for existence. This view defines survival almost entirely in physical terms, focusing on bodies as the primary vehicles through which life persists.

The Theory of Continuity broadens this concept. It suggests that what survives may not be the physical body itself, but the structural organisation of meaning that the body once hosted. In this perspective, the body is a temporary vessel for a much older and more persistent architecture. When the body ceases to function, the structure does not necessarily vanish. Instead, it can remain latent, awaiting conditions in which it can be reassembled and expressed within another individual's mind.

This form of survival is measured not by the replication of genetic sequences, but by the recurrence of semantic configurations. A structure can survive even if no direct biological link connects its earlier and later manifestations. What matters is that the arrangement of semantic atoms and cores retains its coherence and is capable of integration with a new host's cognitive and emotional framework.

Examples of such structural survival appear in cases where specific skills, symbolic patterns, or emotional responses emerge in individuals who have not been exposed to them through conventional learning. A melody, a gesture, a set of associations, or an intuitive grasp of a concept can reappear long after the physical origin of the knowledge has been lost. In these moments, it is not the body that has survived, but the structure of meaning itself.

Survival as a structure requires different conditions from survival as a body. Physical survival depends on nutrition, protection, reproduction, and adaptation to environmental pressures. Structural survival depends on the resilience of the configuration, the strength of its internal connections, and its compatibility with the symbolic and emotional environment in which it re-emerges. A fragile structure, lacking internal coherence, may dissolve quickly when separated from its original host. A robust structure, strongly integrated and charged with emotional or symbolic significance, may persist across lifetimes and contexts.

By recognising this distinction, we are able to see continuity as a process that is not bound to physical inheritance. A person may inherit the genetic material of their parents, but they may also inherit, through entirely different mechanisms, the structures of meaning that originated in other lives, cultures, or even historical periods. In this way, survival extends beyond the body into a wider field of structural persistence.

8.3 Identity as a Recursive System

If survival can occur at the level of structure, then identity must be understood as more than the biological sum of an individual's traits. In the Theory of Continuity, identity is seen as a recursive system, meaning that it continually re-creates itself by drawing upon its own prior states. The process is not linear, beginning at birth and ending at death, but cyclical, with each new expression of identity shaped by patterns established in earlier configurations.

A recursive system functions through repetition and transformation. Each time the system re-emerges, it does so within a new set of circumstances. This new environment may alter the way the structure is expressed, but the underlying architecture remains recognisable. In this way, identity is both stable and adaptive. Stability comes from the persistence of the semantic cores that define the individual's deepest patterns of thought, feeling, and symbolic association. Adaptability comes from the ability of those cores to integrate with new experiences, cultural contexts, and personal relationships.

Recursion also explains why certain aspects of identity may appear stronger or weaker in different manifestations. A semantic core that was central in one life may be peripheral in another if the new environment does not strongly reinforce it. Conversely, a core that was only marginally expressed before may become dominant if the new conditions make it highly relevant. The system is self-referential, but not static. It does not simply repeat the past; it reworks the past into a new present. This view of identity has important implications for understanding human continuity. It suggests that personal identity is not wholly dependent on memory in the conventional sense. A person does not need to recall the narrative of a past life in order to be shaped by it. What matters is that the structural configuration of meaning has been preserved and is active in the present. In many cases, this influence may operate below the threshold of conscious awareness, guiding preferences, talents, emotional reactions, and symbolic responses.

Understanding identity as a recursive system also allows for a more nuanced approach to concepts such as personal growth and transformation. Change is not a departure from the self but a reorganisation of its structural components. Even radical changes in personality or worldview can be understood as new arrangements of persistent cores, activated by the demands and opportunities of a new context.

In this way, the Theory of Continuity reframes identity as a living, evolving structure. It persists not by resisting change, but by continuously re-forming itself in a manner that preserves its essential architecture while allowing for adaptation. This recursive process is what enables identity to survive beyond the limits of a single lifetime and to participate in the broader continuity of human meaning.

PART IV: TOWARD A STRUCTURAL FUTURE

The journey so far has traced a long arc. We began with Darwin, whose work gave humanity its first coherent explanation for the origin and diversification of life. We then turned to the Theory of Continuity, which seeks to explain not only how life begins and changes, but how structures of meaning persist and re-emerge across time. The focus has shifted from the formation of physical bodies to the recurrence of symbolic architectures.

We now ask a different kind of question. If the Theory of Continuity is correct, what does this mean for our future as a species? Evolution by natural selection may have been sufficient to explain our origins, but it may not be enough to account for our destiny. Biology explains how we arrived at our current form. Structure may explain how we endure beyond it.

Here, the concern is not merely with understanding the past or even the present, but with anticipating the paths that continuity might take in the centuries to come. This involves recognising the limitations of a purely biological model and embracing the possibility that identity, meaning, and cultural patterns may survive in ways that transcend the lifespan of individual bodies.

This final part of the book is both a projection and an invitation. It offers a vision of human continuity that builds on Darwin's legacy while moving beyond it. It suggests that to understand the future, we must look not only at our genetic inheritance, but also at the deeper architecture of meaning that we carry forward. In this sense, the Theory of Continuity is not simply an addition to evolutionary thought. It is a framework for imagining the next stage in the story of human existence.

9. Evolution Was Never Enough

Darwin's theory of evolution transformed the way we understand life. By explaining how species emerge, adapt, and diversify through variation, inheritance, and natural selection, it provided a unifying framework for the biological sciences. Yet for all its scope and elegance, it remains a theory of origins and transformation within the material domain. It tells us how forms arise, how they change, and why some persist while others vanish. What it does not address is the persistence of structures that are not material, the continuities that exist in the realm of meaning, memory, and identity.

This section begins from a simple proposition: biology can explain where we come from, but it cannot fully explain why certain configurations of symbolic and cognitive structure reappear across time and context. Evolution has given us the physical apparatus for thought and language, but it does not tell us how particular arrangements of meaning endure beyond an individual lifespan, reactivating in new bodies and new circumstances.

The Theory of Continuity seeks to fill this gap. It proposes that there is another dimension of inheritance, one that operates alongside genetic transmission but follows its own laws. This dimension is not bound to the mechanics of DNA but to the architecture of meaning. Just as genetic traits are shaped by environmental pressures, these symbolic structures are shaped by emotional salience, cultural embedding, and experiential resonance.

In placing evolution and continuity side by side, this section does not seek to replace one with the other. Instead, it argues that the story of human existence is incomplete without both. Darwin's framework illuminates the path of physical formation; the Theory of Continuity adds the path of structural persistence. Together, they offer a more complete account of what it means for a life and the meaning it carries to continue.

9.1 Biology Explains Origin

Darwin's theory of evolution transformed the way we understand the natural world. Before it, the prevailing explanations for the diversity of life were rooted in static creation models or in speculative ideas that lacked a clear mechanism. Darwin offered something different: a dynamic process in which small variations, acted upon by natural selection, accumulate over vast stretches of time to produce the extraordinary variety of forms we see today. In this framework, the origin of any species, including our own, is the result of a long series of adaptations that increased the survival and reproductive success of each generation.

Biology excels at explaining beginnings. It can describe the chemical conditions that allowed life to emerge, the genetic mutations that generated diversity, and the environmental pressures that favoured some traits over others. It can reconstruct the branching patterns of descent that connect all living organisms to common ancestors. This is a remarkable achievement. For the first time in history, humanity could situate itself within the broader tapestry of life, not as an exception to natural processes, but as one expression of them.

The explanatory power of biology is strongest when applied to physical forms. It tells us how bodies come into being, how they change, and how they pass on their traits. It does not, however, by itself, account for the persistence of non-physical structures such as concepts, symbolic systems, and deeply embedded emotional patterns. These forms of continuity do not travel through genetic material, and their recurrence cannot be fully explained by the same mechanisms that shape bones, skin, or organs.

Recognising this limitation does not diminish Darwin's achievement. Instead, it clarifies the scope of what his theory was designed to address. Natural selection is a masterful account of origin, but it was never intended to answer questions about the recurrence of meaning across lifetimes or the survival of structural configurations of thought. To approach those questions, we must consider a complementary model that expands the idea of continuity beyond the purely biological.

9.2 Structure Explains Recurrence

If biology provides an explanation for origin, then structure offers an explanation for recurrence. In the Theory of Continuity, the focus shifts from the creation of physical forms to the re-emergence of symbolic and cognitive architectures. These architectures are made of semantic atoms, the smallest units of meaning, which combine into semantic cores that carry thematic, emotional, and conceptual weight. Over time, these cores become the organising centres of a person's cognitive and symbolic life.

Recurrence occurs when these configurations reappear in a new context, often without any direct transfer of physical material from the original host. In other words, the recurrence of structure does not require the inheritance of DNA. Instead, it relies on the resilience and integrity of the semantic architecture itself. A structure that has achieved sufficient internal coherence and emotional charge can survive beyond the life of its original body, awaiting conditions that allow it to reassemble and express itself again.

This form of continuity can be observed in cases where a person, without any identifiable training or exposure, exhibits skills, knowledge, or symbolic associations that mirror those found in another individual from a different time or place. The emergence of these traits is not random. Rather, it reflects the activation of a pre-existing configuration that has retained its integrity across time. Just as genetic information can remain dormant for generations before reappearing in a physical trait, structural information can remain latent until the right cognitive, cultural, or emotional environment brings it into expression.

The mechanism of recurrence in the structural domain parallels certain aspects of biological inheritance, but it operates in a different medium. In biology, the key material is the genetic code. In structural continuity, the key material is the arrangement of meaning units within a coherent framework. Both are subject to forces that shape their persistence. For genes, these forces include mutation, recombination, and natural selection. For structures, they include symbolic reinforcement, cultural transmission, and emotional salience.

Understanding recurrence through structure allows us to bridge the gap between observed phenomena and theoretical models. Biological evolution accounts for why a body exists in its present form. Structural continuity accounts for why a mind may express patterns, abilities, and symbolic tendencies that are not the product of its present life experiences. In this sense, the Theory of Continuity is not a replacement for Darwinian evolution, but a necessary extension of it, one that explains how patterns of meaning can endure and re-emerge long after the original physical form has disappeared.

9.3 Continuity as the Missing Paradigm

Darwin's theory gave us the most compelling account of how life forms arise, diversify, and adapt. It provided the conceptual foundation for modern biology, reshaping not only science but also philosophy, anthropology, and the way humanity perceives itself. However, its focus remained within the boundaries of physical existence. It explained the origin of form, but not the persistence of form in the absence of its original physical substrate. This is where the Theory of Continuity seeks to extend the conversation.

The missing paradigm is one that unites biological and structural processes into a single vision of human existence. In this paradigm, biological evolution is responsible for the emergence of the body, while structural continuity explains the survival and recurrence of meaning. The two processes are distinct in their mechanisms but parallel in their dynamics. Both involve the creation, retention, and transmission of information. Both are shaped by selective forces. Both produce patterns that persist across time.

Continuity as a paradigm acknowledges that not all that survives is made of flesh and bone. Cultural traditions, symbolic systems, emotional associations, and cognitive architectures can endure just as tenaciously as physical traits. A story, a song, a set of mathematical principles, or an internalised symbolic pattern can pass from one context to another, surviving changes in language, geography, and even the identity of the host mind. In the most striking cases, these structures reappear in ways that suggest a form of persistence not dependent on direct cultural transmission. By integrating structural continuity into the broader framework of evolution, we gain the ability to account for phenomena that have long remained at the margins of scientific explanation. Reports of unlearned skills, spontaneous symbolic expression, or deeply embedded thematic patterns may no longer need to be dismissed as anomalies. Instead, they can be understood as evidence of a structural process that complements biological inheritance.

This paradigm also reframes our understanding of human survival. If identity and meaning can persist as structural configurations, then the human story does not begin and end with the lifespan of the body. Continuity becomes a process that extends beyond the physical, allowing for the reactivation of past structures in new forms. It is in this sense that the Theory of Continuity is not merely an addition to evolutionary thought, but the completion of its logical arc.

Examined jointly, Darwin's theory and the Theory of Continuity form a two-part explanation of human existence: the first describing how we come to be, the second describing how we continue to be. It is this combined vision that opens the way for a deeper and more comprehensive account of what it means to be human.

10. Toward a Structural Future

Every theory reaches a point where its immediate questions give way to larger possibilities. Darwin's work began with the careful observation of variation in living forms and unfolded into a revolutionary framework for understanding the origin of species. The Theory of Continuity begins with the study of how meaning, memory, and identity persist, but it inevitably leads to the question of what these continuities might mean for the future of human understanding.

This section looks ahead to a time when the study of continuity could take its place alongside the life sciences as a recognised field of inquiry. The goal is not only to explain why certain symbolic and cognitive structures reappear, but to apply that knowledge in ways that can benefit individuals and societies. Just as evolutionary theory reshaped fields as diverse as medicine, agriculture, and ecology, a mature science of continuity could influence education, mental health, cultural preservation, and even the design of intelligent systems.

A structural future requires us to think beyond the survival of the body toward the survival of form, pattern, and meaning. It invites a redefinition of what it means to inherit, to adapt, and to evolve. In such a future, the measure of continuity would not be limited to the passing on of genetic material, but would include the enduring influence of ideas, skills, and symbolic frameworks.

In exploring these possibilities, this section is both speculative and practical. It reflects on how the Theory of Continuity might develop as a discipline and on how it could contribute to the broader landscape of human knowledge. It asks what it would mean to live in a world that recognises the persistence of structure as a natural process, and what new responsibilities such recognition would bring.

10.1 What Darwin Might Say Now

If Darwin could join the conversation today, he would find a world transformed beyond anything he could have imagined. The core of his theory still stands, supported by vast bodies of evidence from genetics, palaeontology, and comparative anatomy. Besides, he would also see that the questions facing humanity have shifted. In his century, the great challenge was to explain the diversity of life without appealing to supernatural intervention. In ours, it is to understand how life continues and transforms in ways that are not solely biological.

Darwin might listen to the accounts of people who display unlearned abilities or knowledge they could not have acquired in their current lifetime. He might hear the patterns in their speech, the symbolic images they recall, the coherence of memories that do not belong to the present. His instinct would be to seek a natural explanation, just as he did for the adaptations of finches or the colours of orchids. Yet he would recognise that this realm requires tools beyond those he developed.

The Theory of Continuity would offer him a framework that resonates with his own approach. It is observational, pattern-based, and committed to grounding explanations in natural processes rather than metaphysical claims. He might see in it a parallel to his own work: where he traced the inheritance of physical traits through time, the Theory of Continuity traces the inheritance of symbolic and structural traits. Both rely on the retention of information, both adapt under environmental pressures, and both reveal the remarkable persistence of form.

Darwin's curiosity might lead him to ask whether the same principles that govern the survival of a species could also govern the survival of meaning. He might note that in both cases, what survives is what is able to adapt to changing conditions while maintaining its essential coherence. He might even see in structural continuity an extension of the evolutionary principle into a domain that his own theory did not reach.

Most of all, Darwin might appreciate the humility in recognising that no theory is final. Just as he built upon the work of earlier thinkers, he would expect others to build upon his own. He might not have foreseen the need for a theory of continuity, but he would understand its necessity. In the unfolding story of human knowledge, it would be, to him, a natural next chapter.

10.2 Looking Back and Forward

Looking back, the journey from Darwin's nineteenth-century reflections to the Theory of Continuity reveals a remarkable consistency in the human search for understanding. Both perspectives begin with observation, move through careful reasoning, and arrive at a model that aims to explain not only what is seen, but why it happens. Darwin's work redefined the origins of species and located humanity within the same natural processes that shape all living things. The Theory of Continuity seeks to redefine the persistence of meaning and identity, placing them within processes that are equally natural, even if they operate beyond the limits of biology.

To look back is to recognise the power of gradual shifts in thought. The acceptance of evolutionary theory did not happen overnight; it required decades of debate, refinement, and integration into the sciences. In the same way, the Theory of Continuity will not be adopted instantly. It must pass through the same tests of evidence, coherence, and applicability. The ideas may be new, but the path they must take is familiar.

Looking forward, the implications of merging biological and structural perspectives are profound. It opens the possibility of a more complete understanding of human existence, one that embraces both the formation of life and the endurance of meaning. It invites new questions about the nature of identity, the mechanisms of memory, and the ways in which cultural and symbolic systems evolve. It also suggests new methods of inquiry, combining the empirical rigour of the natural sciences with the interpretive depth of the humanities.

The future shaped by this vision would not discard Darwin's insights but would expand them. Just as his work expanded the scope of natural history beyond the immediate present to encompass the deep past, the Theory of Continuity expands the scope of human understanding to encompass the deep future. It treats the continuity of meaning as a legitimate subject of study, worthy of the same intellectual investment as the continuity of physical form.

In this view, the next stage of human thought is not a rejection of evolution but its completion. The capacity to see life as a structural process, operating across physical and symbolic domains, offers a richer and more resilient framework for understanding who we are and what we might become. This is the bridge between looking back with gratitude and looking forward with curiosity.

10.3 The Humility of Unfinished Theories

Every theory, no matter how transformative, is born into a moment in history. It is shaped by the questions that seem urgent at the time, the tools that are available, and the boundaries of what is considered knowable. Darwin's theory was extraordinary not because it answered every question, but because it asked new ones and offered a framework within which they could be pursued. It reshaped the intellectual landscape while leaving vast territories unexplored.

The Theory of Continuity follows the same path. It does not claim to explain everything about the persistence of meaning, identity, and structure. Rather, it seeks to create a map where there was once only scattered observation and speculation. It offers patterns, models, and possible mechanisms, but it acknowledges that these are starting points, not final destinations. In doing so, it accepts the discipline of humility: the recognition that our explanations are provisional, awaiting the refinement that comes from evidence, dialogue, and time.

Humility in theory-building is not a weakness. It is the acknowledgement that knowledge is a living process. Every insight contains within it the seeds of revision, just as every species contains the seeds of change. Darwin himself understood this. He was careful to note the limits of his evidence, to identify where his reasoning was strongest and where it was weakest, and to encourage others to test his conclusions. His legacy is not only the content of his theory, but also the intellectual posture with which he held it.

For the Theory of Continuity, humility means recognising that some phenomena may never be fully explained, that cultural and symbolic recurrence may involve variables we cannot yet measure, and that new discoveries in neuroscience, anthropology, and linguistics may challenge or transform the framework entirely. It means being open to integration with other disciplines and to the possibility that the next leap forward will come from an unexpected direction. This humility is also a safeguard against the temptation of finality. To declare a theory complete is to close the door on curiosity. To accept it as unfinished is to leave space for future explorers to walk further than we can see. If Darwin could speak now, perhaps he would remind us that the strength of a theory lies not in its claim to perfection, but in its ability to invite further questions.

And so this book ends as it began, with a conversation. Not a conversation that seeks to have the last word, but one that seeks to keep the words moving forward, carried by those who will come after. The Theory of Continuity is offered in that spirit: as a contribution to an unfinished dialogue about human existence, formed in the past, living in the present, and continuing into the uncharted future.

11. From the Theory of Continuity to the Future of Knowledge

The Theory of Continuity proposes that human knowledge and experience are not confined to the biological brain or cultural conditioning but are carried in structural forms that persist across time and circumstance. These forms consist of semantic atoms, the smallest indivisible units of meaning, which cluster into semantic cores and are expressed outwardly through visiblers such as speech, gesture, or artistic creation. Surrounding these elements is the contextual membrane, which regulates their activation, filtering which structures remain latent and which become visible.

Continuity arises because these structures are not destroyed with the dissolution of an individual life or the interruption of consciousness. They remain intact as configurations of meaning, awaiting reactivation when a suitable trigger is present. This explains both the striking recall of detail in Reincarnation cases and the sudden emergence of exceptional skills in Acquired Savant Syndrome. What may appear as inexplicable or supernatural is, within this framework, evidence of structural stability and re-emergence. The central claim of the Theory of Continuity, therefore, is that memory and knowledge are not best understood as stored information but as reactivatable structures of meaning. This perspective redefines phenomena once considered mystical or anomalous as intelligible processes grounded in the persistence and reassembly of semantic forms. It is this redefinition that provides the foundation for extending the theory into practical domains of knowledge, learning, medicine, and technology.

11.1 Artificial Intelligence (AI)

Artificial Intelligence has advanced rapidly in recent decades, yet most current systems remain rooted in statistical learning. They accumulate vast amounts of data and generate outputs through pattern recognition, but their knowledge is essentially additive and surface-level. They do not remember in the human sense, nor do they display genuine creativity or continuity of meaning across different contexts.

The Theory of Continuity suggests an alternative architecture for AI, one that is grounded not in the storage of data but in the reactivation of structural patterns. If semantic atoms, cores, and visiblers form the deep grammar of human cognition, then a truly intelligent machine would need to operate by reassembling such structures rather than by merely retrieving pre-encoded information. Memory, in this model, is not an archive but a set of dormant configurations waiting to be triggered by contextual stimuli.

A hypothetical example illustrates this shift. Imagine an AI trained not on the rote memorisation of millions of sentences but on the structural principles of meaning. When exposed to a new context, such as a child's drawing or a fragment of music, the system does not search a database for the closest match. Instead, it reconstructs semantic cores by aligning latent structures with the cues provided. In doing so, the AI demonstrates a form of reactivation akin to the way humans recall forgotten memories or awaken dormant abilities.

Such an AI would not only process language or images but would also show the capacity for symbolic transfer, where knowledge from one domain re-emerges in another. Just as a musician who suddenly acquires mathematical insight draws upon a shared structural core, the AI could translate between music, geometry, and language in ways that mirror human creativity. This is not mere cross-modal translation but the manifestation of structural continuity across domains.

The implications are profound. An AI built on the principles of semantic continuity would offer new levels of adaptability, generating solutions not by extrapolating from existing data but by reactivating latent structures in response to novel challenges. It would also provide greater transparency, since its reasoning could be traced through identifiable structural pathways rather than opaque statistical weights. Such a system could approach the elusive goal of artificial creativity, not by imitating human expression but by drawing on the same principles of reactivation that govern human thought.

By applying the Theory of Continuity, Artificial Intelligence research can move beyond the limits of current machine learning. It can begin to explore a future in which machines do not simply compute but participate in the structural re-emergence of meaning. In doing so, AI would not only extend human capability but also provide empirical confirmation of continuity as a universal principle of cognition.

11.2 Education

In education, the Theory of Continuity can offer profound insights into why some concepts remain anchored in a learner's mind for decades while others fade within weeks. At the heart of this lies the formation of semantic cores, clusters of meaning bound together through thematic, emotional, and symbolic associations. When teaching strategies deliberately foster such clustering, the learner's engagement moves beyond memorising isolated facts toward embedding knowledge within a resilient structure. This shift changes the quality of learning from temporary recall to enduring mastery.

Understanding the architecture of meaning also makes it possible to address one of the most persistent challenges in education, which is the disconnect between short-term performance, as measured by tests or assignments, and long-term mastery that sustains itself without continuous rehearsal. The Theory of Continuity suggests that concepts are retained when they are reinforced through multiple and varied visiblers such as words, images, gestures, applications, and creative outputs that activate and strengthen the underlying core. An idea taught only in a single context is far more fragile than one encountered across multiple domains of experience, each contributing to a thicker and more permeable contextual membrane.

This perspective also has implications for the sequencing of learning. If certain semantic atoms are introduced early and linked to meaningful emotional or symbolic contexts, they are more likely to be reactivated later in life, even after long periods of dormancy. Such reactivation is not limited to rote memory; it can manifest as intuitive problem-solving, creative synthesis, or the spontaneous recall of cultural and linguistic patterns. In practical terms, this means that curricula could be designed not simply to deliver content but to strategically plant and strengthen the architecture of meaning that will continue to grow, adapt, and re-emerge throughout the learner's life.

By aligning teaching methods with the natural processes of meaning formation, educators could close the gap between what is taught and what is truly learned. In doing so, education would no longer be measured only by the immediate demonstration of knowledge, but by the learner's ability to draw upon and reconfigure that knowledge years later, in entirely new and unforeseen contexts.

11.3 Second Language Acquisition and Bilingualism

The Theory of Continuity offers a new perspective on how individuals acquire and retain a second language over the long term. It suggests that language learning is not solely a process of memorising vocabulary and grammar rules but also a process of constructing and reinforcing semantic cores that integrate meaning, context, and emotional resonance. These cores can remain dormant for years yet retain their structural integrity, allowing them to be reactivated when an individual is re-exposed to the language.

In this view, heritage language learners and long-term bilinguals may retain far more latent knowledge than surface fluency tests suggest. Even after years of non-use, reactivation triggers such as cultural immersion, emotionally significant conversations, or symbolic cues can revive deeply embedded structures of meaning. This explains why some learners can regain a language with remarkable speed after an extended absence, while others struggle despite sustained exposure.

Understanding language learning through the lens of semantic cores has practical implications for curriculum design and pedagogy. Rather than focusing only on repetition and mechanical practice, educators could design experiences that deliberately embed language into emotionally and symbolically rich contexts. Storytelling, role-play, and culturally situated learning can create more resilient semantic structures, reducing the rate of forgetting and increasing the likelihood of spontaneous reactivation in later life.

The Theory of Continuity also offers a framework for explaining code-switching and cross-linguistic transfer. When two languages share overlapping semantic atoms within their cores, the activation of one can facilitate or interfere with the other. This provides a structural explanation for why bilinguals sometimes blend languages in context-dependent ways. By recognising and intentionally working with these shared cores, language teaching could move beyond surface fluency to develop a deeper, more enduring multilingual competence.

11.4 Linguistic Anthropology and Endangered Language Revitalisation

The Theory of Continuity offers a structural approach to understanding why certain languages survive over centuries while others vanish within a generation. In linguistic anthropology, it shifts the focus from recording isolated words or grammar rules toward preserving the deeper semantic cores that give a language its cultural vitality. Every language contains semantic atoms that, when clustered into cores, carry not just vocabulary but also symbolic values, worldviews, and emotional resonances. These cores are sustained and expressed through contextual membranes, which in living communities are formed by rituals, storytelling, and everyday interaction.

For endangered languages, this perspective highlights that revitalisation efforts must go beyond producing dictionaries or teaching basic conversational skills. True revitalisation requires the reactivation of dormant semantic cores within communities. This can be achieved by embedding the language into meaningful social contexts where its symbolic and emotional associations are naturally reinforced. For example, teaching traditional songs, conducting ceremonies, or narrating ancestral stories in the target language can re-establish the contextual membranes that make the language feel alive and relevant.

The Theory of Continuity also has implications for language documentation. Rather than merely archiving linguistic data, documentation projects could aim to map the semantic cores and identify their most resilient reactivation triggers. This would create resources that are not only descriptive but also functional in revitalisation, guiding educators and community leaders in re-establishing the natural conditions for the language's survival.

By aligning revitalisation strategies with the structural mechanics of meaning, the Theory of Continuity bridges academic research with community-led language preservation. It provides a framework for understanding why some revival efforts lead to sustained intergenerational transmission while others fade, offering a path toward preserving the cognitive and cultural continuity embedded in language.

11.5 Forensic Linguistics and Criminal Profiling

The Theory of Continuity provides an additional layer of analytical precision to the study of language in legal and investigative contexts. In forensic linguistics, subtle patterns in word choice, syntax, metaphor use, and thematic preference can reveal stable semantic cores that persist across a person's speech or writing, even when they attempt to disguise their identity. These cores are built from recurring configurations of semantic atoms and are regulated by contextual membranes that shape expression according to situational demands. While a speaker may consciously alter surface features of their communication, the underlying structural patterns often remain detectable.

In criminal profiling, this framework can be applied to identify the latent meaning structures that shape an offender's communication style, narrative construction, and symbolic references. For example, a threatening letter, a ransom note, or an online post may carry traces of thematic and symbolic density that point to specific life experiences, cultural influences, or psychological states. The persistence of these cores across different acts of communication can help link seemingly unrelated messages to the same author or reveal connections between an offender's linguistic behaviour and their personal history.

The model also offers insight into how certain communicative patterns resurface after long periods of inactivity. Just as a dormant semantic core can be reactivated by environmental or emotional triggers, past behavioural and linguistic habits may re-emerge under stress or in emotionally charged situations. This understanding could strengthen investigative interviewing techniques by creating conditions that increase the likelihood of such reactivation, allowing investigators to access deeper layers of meaning and intention.

Beyond authorship analysis, the Theory of Continuity could assist in the interpretation of coded or symbolic language used within criminal networks. Recognising that symbolic systems often evolve yet preserve structural continuity, investigators could track the transformation of a code or jargon across time and context, linking present usage to earlier forms and uncovering networks of association that might otherwise remain hidden.

By grounding forensic analysis in a structural model of meaning persistence, the Theory of Continuity extends the scope of linguistic evidence, offering both investigators and legal practitioners a deeper, more systematic approach to understanding how identity, intention, and meaning endure beneath the surface of language.

11.6 Cognitive Archaeology and Symbolic Evolution

The Theory of Continuity provides cognitive archaeology with a new lens for interpreting the symbolic artefacts of early humans. Traditional analyses often focus on the physical form of artefacts, their materials, or their presumed practical uses. The structural perspective shifts attention to the latent semantic cores these artefacts may have carried within the cultures that produced them. A carved figurine, a painted cave wall, or an arrangement of stones can be understood not only as objects of utility or decoration but as visiblers that express deeply embedded semantic atoms and cores.

In this view, symbolic evolution is not simply the accumulation of more complex artefacts over time but the preservation, modification, and reactivation of structural meaning across generations. The persistence of certain geometric patterns, animal motifs, or ritual objects in disparate archaeological sites suggests that specific semantic cores, once formed, can endure far beyond the lifespan of any individual or single community. These cores can be transmitted through migration, trade, or even independent re-emergence when similar environmental and social triggers occur.

Applying the Theory of Continuity to archaeological interpretation could deepen our understanding of how early symbolic systems contributed to cognitive development. For instance, the repeated depiction of certain animals in Upper Palaeolithic cave art might not only reflect the fauna of the time but also the symbolic density of those creatures within the semantic cores of the culture. Such density would increase the resilience of these symbols, allowing them to survive periods of cultural disruption or geographical displacement.

Moreover, the structural approach opens new possibilities for experimental archaeology. By reconstructing contexts that mirror the original environmental and emotional conditions, researchers could test how certain artefacts or symbols might have reactivated latent meaning for ancient communities. This could bridge the gap between static artefacts and the dynamic cognitive worlds they once inhabited, offering a more holistic understanding of human symbolic evolution.

11.7 Virtual Reality and Immersive Learning Design

The Theory of Continuity provides a conceptual foundation for designing immersive environments that go beyond surface-level simulation. By mapping how semantic atoms combine into cores and how contextual membranes regulate their activation, learning experiences in virtual reality can be structured to evoke deeper and more lasting engagement with knowledge. This means that virtual settings can be intentionally designed to activate latent semantic cores, ensuring that the learner is not merely exposed to information but is interacting with meaning in a way that fosters long-term retention.

In immersive learning environments, the interplay of visual, auditory, and kinaesthetic cues can be orchestrated to mirror the conditions that historically embed knowledge most effectively. For example, a virtual simulation for medical training could not only replicate the physical environment of an operating theatre but also incorporate symbolic elements, emotional triggers, and contextual associations that reinforce the procedural knowledge at a structural level. By embedding multiple layers of contextual membrane cues, designers can facilitate the transfer of learning from the simulated setting to real-world practice.

Virtual reality also offers the possibility of reactivating dormant semantic cores in learners who may have partial or fragmented prior knowledge. For instance, an immersive language learning module could recreate culturally rich contexts in which dormant vocabulary or syntactic patterns are triggered by relevant environmental and emotional stimuli. This approach aligns with the Theory of Continuity's emphasis on reactivation through meaningful context rather than rote repetition.

Furthermore, the theory can guide the design of personalised immersive experiences, where the environment adapts to the learner's own semantic architecture. By identifying which cues are most effective for activating certain types of knowledge, virtual reality could become a highly targeted tool for deep learning, memory rehabilitation, and even cultural immersion. Such an approach moves beyond entertainment-focused VR, positioning immersive technology as a precision instrument for structural knowledge transfer.

11.8 Museum Curation and Cultural Heritage Preservation

The Theory of Continuity offers a powerful framework for curating museum experiences that do more than present artefacts as static objects. By recognising that meaning is carried in semantic atoms, organised into cores, and modulated through contextual membranes, curators can design exhibitions that activate deep cultural and historical connections in visitors. This approach moves heritage preservation beyond the mere safeguarding of physical items and toward the preservation and reactivation of the structures of meaning that these items embody.

In practice, this means arranging exhibitions so that artefacts are not simply displayed in chronological or thematic order but are embedded within rich contextual cues that trigger latent knowledge. For example, an ancient musical instrument could be exhibited alongside recreated soundscapes, oral histories, and symbolic imagery, allowing visitors to engage with its meaning in the same structural context that gave it cultural significance. Such multisensory integration aligns with the Theory of Continuity's emphasis on the interplay between semantic cores and their contextual membranes.

This theoretical lens can also guide the development of interactive and immersive exhibits, where visitors actively participate in meaning-making rather than passively observing. Digital reconstructions, augmented reality overlays, and participatory storytelling can be designed to resonate with visitors' own semantic architectures, enabling them to connect their personal experiences to broader cultural narratives. This not only increases engagement but also enhances the retention of historical and cultural knowledge.

Furthermore, the Theory of Continuity supports the preservation of intangible heritage by emphasising the persistence of symbolic and cognitive structures across generations. Rituals, languages, and artistic traditions can be curated in a way that keeps their semantic cores active within living communities, ensuring continuity even in contexts of migration, displacement, or cultural change. Museums, when guided by this perspective, can become active agents in the reactivation of collective memory, serving as catalysts for cultural resilience and intergenerational connection.

11.9 Musicology and Cross-Cultural Pattern Recognition

The Theory of Continuity provides musicology with a structural framework for understanding why certain melodic, rhythmic, and harmonic patterns appear across cultures and historical periods without direct contact between the communities that produce them. In this view, musical forms are not solely products of cultural transmission or individual creativity but may emerge from latent semantic structures embedded in the cognitive architecture of human meaning-making. These structures can reappear when the right emotional, environmental, or symbolic triggers are present, leading to the independent emergence of similar musical motifs in vastly different contexts.

In practical terms, this perspective encourages musicologists to approach musical analysis as the study of visiblers that originate from deeper semantic cores. For example, the recurrence of pentatonic scales, call-and-response structures, or specific rhythmic groupings in geographically distant societies could be interpreted as evidence of reactivated latent cores shaped by shared human experiences such as communal work, ritual, or storytelling. By mapping these recurring elements, researchers can identify structural constants in human musical expression that transcend cultural boundaries.

Cross-cultural pattern recognition also gains depth when examined through the lens of continuity. Traditional comparative musicology often focuses on tracing historical contact or influence, yet the Theory of Continuity invites inquiry into why certain motifs remain stable for centuries or resurface after long periods of dormancy. This may help explain phenomena such as the preservation of musical fragments across generations, the spontaneous reproduction of ancestral tunes by individuals without formal training, or the structural similarities between ancient ritual music and contemporary popular genres.

The implications for contemporary music research are significant. Ethnomusicologists, cognitive scientists, and composers could collaborate to identify and intentionally work with these enduring structural patterns, creating compositions that resonate more deeply across diverse audiences. Moreover, this framework could enhance therapeutic applications of music by using culturally or emotionally resonant motifs to reactivate dormant cores, thereby facilitating memory retrieval, emotional regulation, and cross-generational connection.

11.10 Neuroaesthetics and Creativity Studies

The Theory of Continuity offers a framework for understanding how artistic inspiration and aesthetic experience can emerge from latent structures of meaning. In this view, creativity is not solely the result of spontaneous invention but often involves the reactivation and reconfiguration of pre-existing semantic cores that have been formed through personal experience, cultural exposure, and inherited symbolic patterns. These cores can persist in dormant form until reawakened by stimuli that align with their thematic, emotional, or symbolic architecture.

In the field of neuroaesthetics, this perspective complements neuroscientific investigations into how the brain responds to art, music, and design by adding a structural explanation for why certain forms resonate so deeply. A work of art or a musical phrase may evoke strong affect not simply because of its sensory qualities, but because it aligns with deeply embedded semantic atoms that form part of the viewer's or listener's cognitive heritage. This alignment activates the contextual membrane, allowing the latent core to become visible through intense emotional or imaginative engagement.

For creativity studies, the theory offers an explanation for the phenomenon of sudden insight, where a solution or artistic idea appears fully formed without deliberate step-by-step reasoning. Such moments may represent the reassembly of semantic atoms into a coherent core under conducive conditions, enabling an idea to emerge in a complete and highly integrated form. Similarly, recurring motifs in an artist's body of work can be seen as expressions of a stable semantic core with high symbolic density, one that continually finds new forms of manifestation across different media and contexts.

This structural understanding of creativity has practical implications. Artists and educators could design environments and practices that deliberately stimulate the reactivation of latent cores, fostering originality by drawing on the deep reservoirs of meaning that reside beneath conscious awareness. It also opens possibilities for therapeutic creativity programmes, where engaging with certain aesthetic forms might help individuals access and express aspects of their identity or memory that have been otherwise inaccessible.

11.11 Transgenerational Memory and Epigenetic Studies

The Theory of Continuity offers a structural perspective on how knowledge, behaviours, and symbolic associations may persist across generations without direct teaching. While epigenetic studies investigate how environmental experiences can alter gene expression and influence descendants, the Theory of Continuity suggests that meaning itself can have a structural continuity that parallels biological transmission. Semantic atoms, once arranged into stable cores, can be re-expressed by subsequent generations when similar environmental or emotional conditions trigger their activation.

In this view, cultural practices, family narratives, and inherited behavioural tendencies can be understood as the re-emergence of latent semantic structures, preserved not only through conscious storytelling but also through patterns embedded in communal rituals, symbols, and modes of expression. These structures may remain dormant until activated by cues in the environment, such as participation in a traditional ceremony, exposure to a specific object, or engagement with a familiar phrase.

This framework aligns with and extends current research in epigenetics, which shows that stress, trauma, and other significant life events can leave molecular traces that shape behaviour in later generations. The Theory of Continuity adds a semantic dimension to this process, proposing that meaning can also be transmitted in a structural form, surviving changes in language, location, or social context. For example, a family that has endured migration or displacement may unconsciously pass down symbolic references to a lost homeland through metaphors, naming practices, or visual motifs, even when the language and geography have shifted.

By integrating structural meaning analysis with biological and psychological research, the Theory of Continuity opens new possibilities for understanding how cultural and personal identity persists. It suggests that the intergenerational transmission of meaning is not only a matter of memory in the traditional sense but also the reactivation of deeply embedded semantic architectures. Such an approach could enrich therapeutic practices aimed at addressing inherited trauma, as well as anthropological studies of cultural resilience and adaptation.

The future of knowledge may lie in bridging the gap between the physical and the symbolic, the material and the immaterial. ASL is one such bridge. By identifying the smallest structural units of meaning and tracing how they cluster, embed, and re-emerge, it gets us a precise yet adaptable language for describing continuity. This structural approach can unite fields that have traditionally been separated by methodology, creating a shared platform for understanding how meaning survives.

If the nineteenth century was defined by the science of origins, the twenty-first may be defined by the science of continuities. The questions that lie ahead are not only about how life began, but about how the architectures of meaning that define us will endure, transform, and shape the generations yet to come. The Theory of Continuity and the ASL model do not claim to close this inquiry. Instead, they act as a framework and an invitation. They light the path forward, encouraging others to build upon the foundations, to refine the tools, and to imagine more fully the possibilities of what it means to continue.

In conclusion, the work of ASL and the Theory of Continuity is not an endpoint. It is a beginning. Every structure of meaning that we uncover is both a discovery and a question. If continuity is a real and measurable phenomenon, then the challenge is no longer whether it exists, but how far it reaches, how it can be mapped, and how it can be applied to the betterment of human life. This is an open field, one that will demand patience, collaboration, and a willingness to cross the boundaries between disciplines that have too often worked in isolation.

The journey ahead is not simply about preserving knowledge. It is about understanding the architecture of the human mind as a dynamic, evolving system of meaning that transcends the limits of a single lifetime. To walk this path is to accept that the story of human continuity is still being written, and that every generation has the opportunity to shape the next chapter.

11.12 Memory Rehabilitation and Therapy

In memory rehabilitation and therapy, the Theory of Continuity offers a new way of understanding the resilience of meaning after injury, trauma, or cognitive decline. Instead of assuming that memory is simply a storehouse of discrete facts that can be permanently lost, this perspective recognises that the architecture of meaning can survive even when surface-level recall appears to have deteriorated. Semantic atoms and the cores they form may remain dormant within the mind, shielded by layers of the contextual membrane, waiting for the right conditions to emerge again.

This means that therapy does not need to focus exclusively on re-teaching skills in a linear fashion. It can instead work to identify latent cores and activate them through targeted cues, symbolic associations, and emotionally resonant contexts. A familiar song, the scent of a particular spice, the texture of a well-known fabric, or a phrase in a long-forgotten language can act as reactivation triggers, releasing intact structures of meaning that reconnect the individual to their memories, abilities, and sense of self. These triggers work because they bypass the damaged pathways of explicit recall and access the deeper and often more resilient network of meaning.

For individuals recovering from brain injury, this approach can restore functional skills more quickly by tapping into pre-existing cores rather than building entirely new ones from scratch. In the case of degenerative conditions such as dementia, it may prolong the period of functional recall, allowing people to maintain vital connections to their identity, relationships, and life history. Even when full restoration is not possible, reactivated cores can provide islands of clarity, emotional comfort, and meaningful engagement, which in turn can improve quality of life and emotional stability.

By treating memory as a structural phenomenon rather than merely a collection of isolated facts, the Theory of Continuity reframes rehabilitation as an act of reconnection rather than replacement. This approach respects the complexity of the human mind, recognising that the continuity of meaning can survive beyond the apparent limits of memory, and that with the right keys, these hidden rooms of the mind can be unlocked again.

11.13 Dementia Care

In dementia care, the Theory of Continuity provides a framework for understanding why certain memories and abilities can remain intact even as others deteriorate. While conventional approaches often focus on cognitive decline as a uniform loss of memory, the Theory of Continuity suggests that not all meaning is lost at the same rate or in the same way. Semantic cores, which are clusters of meaning formed through strong thematic, emotional, or symbolic associations, may persist long after surface-level recall and language have been impaired. These cores can retain their structure even when the surrounding contextual membranes have been weakened, creating opportunities for targeted reactivation.

From a neurological perspective, this is consistent with research showing that different memory systems degrade unevenly. The hippocampus and temporal lobes, which underpin episodic and declarative memory, are among the earliest regions affected in Alzheimer's disease. Yet circuits associated with music, rhythm, and procedural memory, such as those in the basal ganglia and cerebellum, often remain relatively intact until later stages. This helps to explain why patients who no longer recognise family members may still sing childhood hymns, recite prayers, or tap in rhythm to familiar melodies. ASL reframes this resilience structurally: emotionally and symbolically dense semantic cores are preserved even when the contextual membranes that normally mediate access have thinned or fractured.

Illustrative cases highlight this continuity. A patient unable to recall the names of her children could nonetheless hum lullabies she once sang to them, reactivating not only melodic memory but also the emotional core of maternal attachment. Another individual, though unable to describe his life history, would reach instinctively for his rosary beads and begin to pray, showing that religious rituals clustered around symbolic atoms can persist as intact cores despite severe cognitive decline. In both cases, what appears from a clinical perspective as patchy memory loss is better understood structurally as selective survival and reactivation of semantic cores that carry strong emotional and symbolic density.

This perspective opens the possibility of designing interventions that aim not only to stimulate general cognitive function but to deliberately trigger latent cores through carefully chosen cues. Music, familiar scents, tactile sensations, photographs, or the rhythms of a spoken phrase can act as reactivation triggers, unlocking preserved structures of meaning and reconnecting individuals to fragments of their identity. Such triggers work because they do not rely solely on conscious recall. Instead, they interact directly with the emotional and symbolic architecture of the mind, bypassing the damaged pathways that impede conventional memory retrieval.

In practice, this approach could transform dementia care into a more personalised and humane process. Rather than using generic memory exercises, caregivers could map a patient's life history to identify the semantic atoms and cores most likely to remain accessible. These might be linked to early childhood experiences, deeply ingrained cultural rituals, or long-held personal values. The therapeutic aim would be to weave these preserved cores into daily interaction, maintaining engagement and emotional well-being even as other cognitive functions decline. For instance, a personalised playlist could provide daily stimulation of resilient musical cores, or a symbolic object such as a wedding ring could be used as a stable anchor for conversation and reassurance.

The Theory of Continuity also reframes the goal of dementia treatment. Instead of focusing exclusively on restoring what has been lost, it encourages sustaining what remains structurally intact. By prioritising the preservation and reactivation of core meanings, this method may help to extend the period during which individuals can participate meaningfully in relationships, recognise aspects of their environment, and maintain a sense of self. In doing so, it offers not only a clinical pathway but also a profound ethical commitment to honour the enduring structures of meaning that persist within the human mind, even when much else has faded.

11.14 Stroke Rehabilitation and Aphasia Recovery

The Theory of Continuity offers a fresh perspective on stroke rehabilitation and the recovery of language after brain injury, particularly in cases of aphasia. Traditional rehabilitation often relies on structured repetition, vocabulary drills, and compensatory communication strategies. While these methods can yield improvement, they sometimes overlook the latent structures of meaning that remain intact despite damage to the overt mechanisms of speech production or comprehension.

Within the framework of the Theory of Continuity, language is not merely a set of learned words and grammar rules. It is the outward manifestation of deeper semantic cores, built from semantic atoms and shaped by emotional and symbolic associations. Even when the physical pathways for verbal expression are impaired, the underlying semantic cores may persist, awaiting reactivation. This insight is consistent with clinical observations. For instance, patients with expressive aphasia may be unable to name a cup but still know how to use it appropriately, demonstrating that the conceptual core remains intact even when verbal access is blocked. In a similar way, many patients who cannot speak fluently can nevertheless sing familiar phrases when guided by rhythm and melody, as observed in Melodic Intonation Therapy.

Therapy informed by this model would therefore focus not simply on rebuilding vocabulary, but on stimulating intact semantic cores through symbolic cues, emotionally resonant contexts, and multi-sensory prompts that resemble the original conditions in which the cores were formed. Rather than beginning with generic word lists, a therapist might introduce words, images, and sounds connected to the patient's most deeply embedded experiences. These could include family rituals, personal achievements, or culturally significant symbols. By engaging the emotional and symbolic dimensions of meaning, this approach increases the likelihood of core reactivation, which in turn facilitates more rapid and sustainable restoration of language abilities.

From a neuroscientific perspective, this method resonates with evidence on neuroplasticity. Repeated activation of preserved semantic cores through alternative pathways such as musical, gestural, or sensory channels can encourage the formation of new connections around damaged areas. This reinforces language recovery in a structurally coherent way. The Theory of Continuity, therefore, positions aphasia therapy not only as a technical process of skill retraining, but also as the deliberate reawakening of dormant structures of mind and meaning.

The model also encourages interdisciplinary collaboration between neurologists, speech and language therapists, and cognitive psychologists. This integrated approach allows rehabilitation to address both the mechanics of speech and the architecture of meaning. By treating recovery as a reconnection to identity through the continuity of semantic cores, this framework reframes stroke rehabilitation as both a clinical and ethical endeavour: to restore not only the ability to communicate, but also the deeper structures of self-expression that make language fundamentally human.

11.15 Trauma Recovery and PTSD Treatment

The Theory of Continuity provides a novel framework for understanding and addressing the persistence of traumatic memories in post-traumatic stress disorder (PTSD). In many cases of PTSD, the challenge is not simply that distressing memories exist, but that they remain highly accessible, emotionally charged, and resistant to integration into a coherent life narrative. Conventional therapeutic approaches often aim to desensitise the individual to these memories or to reframe them through cognitive restructuring. While these methods can offer relief, they do not always account for the deeper structural organisation of meaning that underlies traumatic recall.

According to the Theory of Continuity, experiences are encoded into semantic cores that integrate emotional, symbolic, and sensory information. Traumatic events can form cores of exceptionally high symbolic density, with strong emotional salience acting as a powerful reactivation trigger. As a result, even minor environmental cues can cause these cores to resurface vividly, bypassing the individual's sense of control.

A trauma-informed application of this model would focus on carefully modulating the contextual membrane around the traumatic core. This involves creating safe, emotionally neutral contexts in which elements of the traumatic memory can be engaged without overwhelming the individual. Symbolic and sensory cues can be introduced in graduated ways, allowing for gradual reconfiguration of the core so that its meaning shifts from one of immediate threat to one of integrated past experience.

Furthermore, by identifying latent, non-traumatic cores that were active before or alongside the trauma, therapy can work to strengthen these alternative structures of meaning. This provides the individual with stable reference points for identity and self-perception, reducing the dominance of the traumatic core in daily life.

In this way, the Theory of Continuity reframes PTSD treatment not solely as a process of erasing or suppressing unwanted memories, but as a structural rebalancing. It is the deliberate reshaping of the architecture of meaning so that the individual's sense of self is no longer governed by the unfiltered reactivation of a single, overpowering core.

11.16 Neurodevelopmental Disorders (Autism Spectrum, Language Delay)

The Theory of Continuity offers a structural perspective that can complement existing approaches to understanding and supporting individuals with neurodevelopmental conditions such as autism spectrum disorder and language delay. Traditional models often focus on deficits in social interaction, communication, or adaptive functioning. While these descriptions are important for diagnosis, they do not fully account for the distinctive ways in which meaning is formed, stored, and expressed in these conditions.

From the standpoint of the Theory of Continuity, the development of meaning is mediated by the interaction between semantic atoms, semantic cores, and their surrounding contextual membranes. In autism, for example, semantic atoms may cluster into highly specialised or narrowly focused cores, with strong internal coherence but limited porosity to broader social or situational contexts. This can explain why individuals may demonstrate exceptional expertise or memory in specific domains while finding it challenging to generalise those skills to other settings.

In cases of language delay, the formation of semantic cores may occur at a slower pace or follow atypical pathways, with certain contextual membranes remaining overly restrictive. As a result, access to and expression of stored meaning can be delayed, even when the underlying conceptual understanding is present.

By applying the Theory of Continuity, intervention strategies can be designed to gradually adjust membrane porosity in a controlled and supportive way. For autism, this might involve creating bridges between specialised cores and more general social contexts, using familiar and motivating content as the connecting structure. For language delay, therapy could focus on stimulating dormant or partially formed cores through rich, multimodal input that reinforces both the semantic atoms and their contextual links.

This structural approach shifts the focus from attempting to replace atypical patterns of meaning-making with standardised norms, toward recognising and working with the individual's existing architecture of meaning. By doing so, it opens possibilities for more personalised, respectful, and effective pathways to communication and cognitive growth.

11.17 Palliative Care and End-of-Life Communication

The Theory of Continuity offers palliative care a deeper framework for understanding and supporting the emotional, cognitive, and symbolic needs of individuals at the end of life. In such settings, communication often extends beyond the exchange of factual information to include symbolic gestures, emotionally charged words, and shared rituals that hold deep personal significance. These are expressions of semantic cores that may have been formed decades earlier, often linked to formative relationships, cultural traditions, or profound life experiences.

Recognising these expressions as visiblers emerging from enduring semantic structures allows practitioners to approach end-of-life communication with greater sensitivity. A familiar phrase, a piece of music, or even the presence of a specific object can serve as a reactivation trigger, enabling the person to reconnect with long-held memories and aspects of identity that may be otherwise inaccessible due to illness or cognitive decline. This not only supports emotional comfort but can also foster a sense of continuity and coherence in a person's life story during their final days.

In practice, palliative care teams could use the Theory of Continuity to design communication strategies that go beyond generic comfort measures, identifying and working with the individual's unique semantic cores. This might involve revisiting cherished narratives, recreating meaningful sensory environments, or engaging in rituals that symbolically link the person's present experience to significant moments in their past. Such approaches could help alleviate existential distress, reduce feelings of isolation, and promote a more peaceful transition.

Furthermore, the theory's focus on structural persistence highlights the importance of intergenerational exchanges at the end of life. Conversations, stories, and symbolic acts shared between the person and their loved ones can carry latent semantic content that survives beyond the individual's death, continuing to influence the emotional and symbolic lives of those who remain. In this way, palliative care informed by the Theory of Continuity not only attends to the individual but also participates in the transmission of meaning across lifetimes.

11.18 Pain Management and Psychosomatic Medicine

The Theory of Continuity provides a framework for understanding the complex interplay between mind, meaning, and bodily experience that lies at the heart of pain management and psychosomatic medicine. While conventional approaches often separate the biological mechanisms of pain from its psychological and social dimensions, the Theory of Continuity views pain as an experience that is both neurologically encoded and structurally embedded within patterns of meaning.

In this view, the persistence of pain is not only the result of ongoing physical injury or dysfunction but can also arise from the reactivation of semantic cores associated with previous trauma, illness, or distress. These cores may hold symbolic and emotional associations that amplify or sustain the subjective experience of pain even after the original cause has resolved. The contextual membrane surrounding such cores regulates how readily pain-related meanings are triggered by environmental cues, emotional states, or interpersonal interactions.

In psychosomatic conditions, physical symptoms often emerge without a clear organic cause, reflecting the embodiment of unresolved or latent meaning structures. The Theory of Continuity suggests that these symptoms are not arbitrary but are manifestations of visiblers linked to deeply encoded semantic cores. Addressing them requires working with both the structural content of these cores and the contexts that sustain their activation.

Therapeutic approaches informed by this model could combine conventional pain management with targeted symbolic interventions. This might involve guided imagery, narrative reframing, or the use of meaningful sensory cues to alter the porosity of the membrane around pain-related cores, reducing their activation frequency and intensity. In psychosomatic presentations, the goal would be to identify and work through the underlying structural meanings so that their physical manifestations diminish naturally.

By integrating the structural insights of the Theory of Continuity into pain and psychosomatic care, practitioners could develop strategies that treat not just the symptom but the architecture of meaning that sustains it, opening the way to more enduring relief and a restoration of the individual's sense of agency over their own body.

11.19 Intercultural Communication

In intercultural communication, the Theory of Continuity offers a structural explanation for why some ideas, stories, and symbols are understood across vastly different cultural settings, while others remain inaccessible or easily misunderstood. It recognises that beneath the surface differences in language and custom, there are deep-seated semantic atoms and cores that can be shared between cultures, even when the surrounding contextual membranes differ greatly. These structural commonalities allow certain meanings to be recognised intuitively, creating moments of instant connection despite the absence of shared vocabulary or history.

For example, a gesture of nurturing, the symbolism of light overcoming darkness, or the emotional force of a reunion scene in a story may resonate across cultural boundaries because the underlying semantic core is present in many human experiences. The challenge in intercultural communication lies not in creating meaning from nothing but in identifying where such latent cores already exist, and then activating them through forms that are intelligible within the target cultural context.

The Theory of Continuity also helps to explain why certain attempts at cross-cultural communication fail, even when the language used is technically correct. If the semantic core in one culture is wrapped in a highly specific and opaque contextual membrane, its meaning may not pass easily into another cultural system without careful adaptation. This is often the case when symbols or narratives rely on references that are deeply embedded in local history, religion, or social practice.

In practical terms, applying the Theory of Continuity to intercultural communication means learning to map the semantic structures of both the sender and receiver. This involves identifying the atoms and cores that are most likely to overlap, and deliberately selecting visiblers, whether words, images, gestures, or rituals that can travel across membranes without losing their essential meaning. It also means understanding when translation must go beyond literal substitution, reconfiguring the form of expression so that it interacts successfully with the contextual membrane of the receiving culture.

By framing cultural exchange in terms of structural continuity, this approach shifts the focus from overcoming difference to uncovering connection. It recognises that communication is most successful when it works with the architectures of meaning that already exist, allowing each culture to activate in the other what is already latent within it. This makes intercultural dialogue not a process of imposing new ideas, but one of reawakening shared human cores that have been shaped by different histories yet remain capable of mutual recognition.

11.20 Cross-Cultural Anthropology and Comparative Mythology

The Theory of Continuity provides a structural lens for examining the persistence and recurrence of cultural symbols, myths, and rituals across widely separated societies. It proposes that certain semantic cores, once formed within a cultural context, can be preserved in latent form and reactivated in new generations or entirely different cultural settings when similar symbolic or environmental triggers occur. This perspective moves beyond the assumption that all similarities must result from direct contact or borrowing.

By focusing on the internal architecture of meaning rather than the external form alone, the theory offers an explanation for why archetypes such as the flood narrative, the world tree, or the hero's journey appear in geographically distant and historically disconnected traditions. These recurring motifs may represent reconfigurations of similar underlying semantic atoms that cluster into stable cores with high symbolic density, making them resilient to loss and more likely to reappear across time.

For anthropologists and mythologists, this approach provides a tool for mapping symbolic continuities across cultures without reducing them to coincidence or universal human psychology in the abstract. It invites researchers to investigate the contextual membranes surrounding these cores, exploring how social, environmental, and emotional factors modulate their expression in specific cultural settings.

This framework could also help explain why some cultural elements vanish rapidly while others endure for millennia. A myth or ritual with low symbolic density may fade quickly, while those with deeply interwoven semantic atoms are more resistant to erosion, even when their original social context has disappeared. By identifying and tracing these deep structures, scholars may better understand the mechanisms through which human symbolic heritage is preserved, transformed, and renewed.

EPILOGUE

The Conversation Continues

In writing this book, I have often imagined Darwin sitting across from me, listening as I lay out the patterns and possibilities that have emerged from my work. I imagine him with the same attentive patience he showed toward the finches, barnacles, and beetles that so captivated him, weighing each idea with care before offering his thoughts. I do not know what he would accept, what he would question, or what he would challenge outright. But I believe he would recognise the spirit in which this theory is offered, a spirit that values evidence, welcomes debate, and refuses to settle for easy answers.

The Theory of Continuity is not an attempt to replace Darwin's work. It is an attempt to stand alongside it, to extend the reach of evolutionary thinking into a realm he could not fully explore. Where his focus was the formation of life, mine is its continuation in forms that are not limited to the body. We are shaped by biology, but we are also shaped by the structures of meaning that live within us, carried across time by memory, culture, and perhaps processes we do not yet fully understand.

This book has traced the arc from formation to continuity, from the mechanics of natural selection to the persistence of symbolic and structural forms. Along the way, it has explored how identity can survive the body, how meaning can be reactivated in new contexts, and how the threads of human existence are woven from both physical and symbolic strands.

If there is one truth that remains clear to me at the end of this journey, it is that no single theory can hold all the answers. Knowledge moves forward through conversation, across centuries, across disciplines, across the lives of those who ask and those who answer. This book is part of that ongoing conversation, and I hope it will invite others to join it.

I offer the Theory of Continuity not as a conclusion, but as a beginning. It is a framework to be tested, refined, and perhaps even overturned. What matters most is that the questions it raises continue to be asked. The search for understanding is not a path with a final destination; it is a movement without end, shaped by every mind that dares to look beyond what is known.

In the end, Darwin's greatest gift was not simply his explanation of evolution. It was his example: the courage to observe with honesty, the patience to think with care, and the humility to know that the story is never finished. That is the conversation I hope to continue. That is the conversation I now pass on to you.

Toward a New Science of Continuity

The Theory of Continuity began as an attempt to address a very specific puzzle: why certain patterns of meaning, identity, and ability seem to survive the loss of the body and emerge again in entirely new circumstances. Over time, it became clear that this puzzle could not be contained within the boundaries of a single discipline. The implications of continuity extend far beyond the original question and invite a fundamental rethinking of how we understand human inheritance, memory, and the evolution of knowledge.

198

To treat continuity as a scientific subject is to challenge the prevailing boundaries of what is considered measurable. It asks science to look not only at what can be observed in the laboratory, but also at patterns that appear across cultures, generations, and even lifetimes. It does not reject the standards of empirical method; rather, it extends them into areas that have traditionally been dismissed as anecdotal, too complex, or beyond the reach of current instrumentation.

A genuine science of continuity would be inherently interdisciplinary. It would require linguistics to engage with neuroscience, allowing the study of meaning to be grounded in the realities of brain architecture. Anthropology would contribute insights into how symbolic systems are embedded within cultural practices, while cognitive psychology would provide tools for analysing how structures of thought are formed, retained, and reactivated. Evolutionary biology would be invited to reconsider its models, taking into account the possibility that inheritance can be structural as well as genetic. Such a collaboration would dissolve the silos that keep disciplines apart, replacing them with a shared vocabulary for understanding how meaning survives.

This emerging science would also need new tools. These might include methods for mapping the recurrence of symbolic patterns across time and space, databases that track the reappearance of rare semantic structures, and analytical frameworks that can distinguish between accidental similarity and structural reactivation. Longitudinal studies could be designed to follow individuals who display spontaneous knowledge or abilities, while historical and ethnographic data could be mined for recurring configurations of meaning that transcend individual experience.

At its core, this science would require a shift in perspective. Survival would no longer be defined solely as the continuation of genetic material. Instead, it would encompass the persistence of meaning itself, carried in the architecture of semantic cores and activated under the right conditions. The focus would move from the survival of the fittest organism to the survival of the most resilient structures of mind. Emotional salience, symbolic density, and cultural embedding would be studied as forces that give certain structures the power to endure, even in the absence of the original biological host.

The potential applications of such a science are profound. In education, it could shed light on why certain concepts seem to be grasped intuitively by some learners but require great effort for others. In therapy, it could offer new ways of understanding trauma, not only as a wound that must be healed, but as a powerful structural event that shapes how meaning is organised and expressed. In the arts, it could explain the mysterious sense of familiarity that some people feel when encountering a style, a melody, or a story from a culture they have never experienced. Even in artificial intelligence, it could inform the design of systems that replicate not only the processing of information, but the continuity of structured meaning across contexts.

A new science of continuity would not replace Darwin's legacy, but extend it. Darwin showed how physical forms evolve through variation, selection, and inheritance. The Theory of Continuity applies these principles to the evolution of meaning, revealing that the architecture of thought is also shaped by forces of selection and retention. Where biology traces the lineage of bodies, continuity traces the lineage of structures that give rise to identity, culture, and the sense of self.

By recognising that evolution has both a physical and a structural dimension, this science would take a decisive step toward unifying the study of life and mind. It would acknowledge that to understand what it means to be human, we must look not only at the body that carries us, but also at the patterns of meaning that define who we are, and who we have been before.

APPENDICES
Appendix A: Summary of Key Concepts

- Continuity: The persistence of structural meaning across time, contexts, or lifetimes.

- Latent Structure: A semantic configuration held in dormant form until reactivated.

- Latent Identity: The structural continuity of meaning within an individual or across lifetimes.

- Symbolic Density: The concentration of meaning within a symbolic form, increasing its resilience to loss or distortion.

- Reactivation Trigger: An environmental, emotional, or symbolic stimulus that prompts the re-expression of a latent core.

- Semantic Atom: The smallest indivisible unit of meaning within the Theory of Continuity, carrying a distinct conceptual or symbolic value.

- Semantic Core: A cluster of semantic atoms linked by thematic, emotional, or symbolic association, forming a stable structure of meaning.

- Contextual Membrane: The surrounding layer that regulates the interaction between a semantic core and its environment, determining when and how the core is expressed.

- Visibler: The observable manifestation of a semantic core, such as speech, gesture, artistic creation, or other expressive acts.

- Structural Inheritance: The transmission of meaning structures independent of genetic material, enabling continuity across lifetimes or cultural boundaries.

- Membrane Porosity: The extent to which a contextual membrane allows external cues to activate a latent semantic core.

- Cross-modal Expression: The reappearance of a semantic core in a different expressive medium from its original form, such as a verbal memory emerging in music or art.

- Semantic Reactivation Loop: The recurring cycle in which a latent semantic core becomes active, is expressed through visiblers, and may return to dormancy until triggered again.

- Symbolic Resonance: The amplification of a semantic core's activation when its symbolic content aligns with emotionally charged or culturally significant contexts.

- Symbolic Loop: A recurring cycle in which a particular image, phrase, gesture, or idea triggers an emotional response.

- Semantic Gravity: the attractive force by which certain cores (especially emotionally charged or symbolically dense ones) draw atoms into stable configurations and persist across time.

- Membrane Porosity: the degree to which a contextual membrane allows expression; thin membranes are highly porous, thick membranes restrict expression.

- Membrane Types: membranes may be homogeneous (consistent across contexts) or inhomogeneous (variable depending on situation, culture, or emotion). Membranes may be thin, allowing semantic cores to surface with clarity and force, or thick, filtering expression so that only fragments or impressions emerge.

- Core Reactivation Loop: the cyclical process by which dormant cores are reactivated through triggers, often across time, trauma, or lifetimes.

- Structural Continuity: the persistence of semantic cores beyond the lifespan of the individual, forming the basis of continuity in Reincarnation or savant cases.

- Semiotic Density: the degree of symbolic compression within a core, which increases its stability and likelihood of re-emergence (e.g., idioms, metaphors, rituals).

- Latent Knowledge: knowledge encoded structurally in cores but not consciously accessible until triggered.

- Structural Adaptation: the way cores reconfigure when expressed in a new cultural or material context (e.g., a ritual act becoming an artistic motif).

- Invisible Core: The Invisible Core is the irreducible essence of meaning that lies beneath expression. It is not directly observable but shapes how semantic atoms combine and how semantic cores form. The core acts as the organising centre of meaning, carrying the potential for reactivation across time and context. Although it cannot be spoken or written in its pure form, it becomes visible through visiblers such as words, gestures, symbols, or actions that give partial expression to its hidden structure. The Invisible Core is therefore both the anchor of stability in meaning and the source of its re-emergence.

Appendix B: Theory of Evolution vs Theory of Continuity

Dimension	Darwin's Theory of Evolution	Theory of Continuity
Domain	Physical and biological forms	Symbolic, cognitive, and structural forms
Unit of Transmission	Genetic material (DNA)	Semantic atoms and cores
Mechanism of Change	Variation, natural selection, and inheritance	Combination, retention, and reactivation
Environment	Physical world: predators, climate, resources	Symbolic world: experiences, relationships, cultural contexts
Time Scale	Generational, over millions of years	Lifespan to cross-lifetime; potentially instantaneous reactivation

Forces of Selection	Survival and reproductive advantage	Emotional salience, symbolic resonance, cultural embedding
Evidence Base	Fossil records, comparative anatomy, genetics	Cross-lifetime case studies, linguistic analysis, symbolic pattern mapping
Goal of the Model	Explain the origins and diversification of life	Explain the recurrence and persistence of meaning and identity

Appendix C: Poster at Postgraduate Research Showcase 2013

ATOMIC STRUCTURE IN LINGUISTICS

Luong Van Nhan - Ph.D Researcher
Department of English - Faculty of Humanities
University of Southampton
Email: nvl1e11@soton.ac.uk

1. INTRODUCTION

Aiming to introduce a new point of view, my study, supposing the common structure of all languages, takes the Atomic Structure in Chemistry to apply in drawing the general image of a unit of information in Linguistics.

2. STRUCTURE OF A UNIT OF INFORMATION

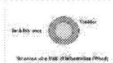

This study examines Word, in the same formation of an Atom, appearing to us with its *visible part* which is from now named *Visibler*, then comes to our mind with its *nucleus - Invisible core*.

For example, *WHERE* is a word as well as a unit of information, appearing to us with its *visible part* formed of five letters w h e r e, touching our mind with its *nucleus* embedded the meaning of *place*. In other words, the *Visibler* is w h e r e, and the *Invisible core* is *place*.

3. STRUCTURE OF VISIBLER

The *Visibler* of a unit of information in any language is always formed by the connection of the *Basic grains*.

* In Latin-Alphabet languages, *basic grains* are the *Letters*, a, b, c, etc. for example, the *Visibler* of the word *Independence* is the series of 12 grains (letters) I n d e p e n d e n c e

* In Symbolic languages, *basic grains* are the *Characters*; for example, the word *Love* in Chinese language 愛 has its *Visibler* formed of 10 grains (characters) ノ 一 爫 冖 凵 心 夊 愛

The *Basic grains* of a unit of information never run freely in the *Visibler*, but always operate in two main directions.

* First, if the unit of information is in focus of monosyllabic, for instance, *bee, man, cheap...* in English, or *ba (father), mẹ (mother), bún (soup)...* in Vietnamese, or *一 (one)* in Chinese, basic grains (letters and characters) stand individually but inseparably in the meaningful and visible form.

 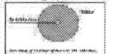

* Second, if the information unit is in multisyllabic form, *basic grains* tend to stay in groups.

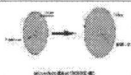

In English language, *basic grains (letters)* prefer grouping at morphemic one, then, each of them will connect each other to make full version of a unit. For example, the 13 letters functioning as 13 *basic grains* in the *Visibler* of the word *unconformably* u n c o n f o r m a b l y which do not stand by their own but run into group of morphemes as follows: [u-n] + [c-o-n-n] + [f-o-r-m] + [a-b-l] + [l-y].

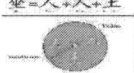

In Chinese language, most of the words (units of information) are formed of more than two characters which often stay in pairs of groups before getting to be in full version of a unit. For example, the word 王 or, in its *Visibler*, is the combination of 7 characters which do not stay separately but in three groups: 坐 = 人 + 人 + 土, each of which is already an independent syllable.

$$坐 = 人 + 人 + 土$$

4. THE MOVING OF BASIC GRAINS IN VISIBLER

The *Visibler* always comes to our eyes in a united form although it is actually structured of *basic grains* which have two main kinds of appearance: standing individually and forming into groups (morphemic group in English or syllabic group in Vietnamese, etc).

* Firstly, if the unit is a monosyllabic version, each *basic grain* has a fixed and logical position in the linking to the others. For example, the unit [word] *xin* in Vietnamese (English equivalent is *please*) has three *basic grains*: x - i - n in which the position of grain x is at the middle, grain i must stand to the left side and grain n is on the right side of x (in terms of *convened out way*). In terms of *left-to-right view*, position of grains is x, i, n and in x, which could be vice versa in terms of *right-to-left observation*.

* Secondly, if the unit is in the form of multi-syllable version, the moving of *basic grains* can be classified in three types:

→ In English language, the structure of a multi-syllable word is often in the formula: *prefix-root-suffix. Root* functions as the central part fixing its stand and, like a magnet, pulling *prefix* close to its left side and *suffix* to its right side. *Basic grains*, in this case, belong to root-oriented moving. For example, there are 10 *basic grains* in the word *undividable*: u-n-d-i-v-i-d-a-b-l-e which orients to form prefix *[u-n]*, suffix *[a-b-l-e]* and root *[v-a-l-e]*. The moving of these *basic grains* is the orientation to the Root: *[u-n]* → *[v-a-l-e]* ← *[a-b-l-e]*

→ In Vietnamese language, multi-syllable form is often structured of two, three or four independent syllables which have relative independence in connecting to each other to form a united unit of information. The syllables in Vietnamese language stand separately to the others in the *Visibler*. They carry out both actions at the same time, *pushing* (push the other syllable to get the distance) and *pulling* (pull to keep close enough to form the unity of words). Therefore, the moving of *basic grains* in Vietnamese is the *relative pushed-pulled moving*. For example, the word *xe ôtô* (an English equivalent is *car*) is a single unit of information structured of two independent syllables. The first one has three *basic grains*: x - e, and the second one has the same number of *basic grains*: ô - i - ô → *[x-e]* ← → *[ô-t-ô]*

→ In Chinese language, syllables do not stand separately, they tend to co-exist close together to set a new form of the unit of information. This kind of moving is named *constructed moving*. For example, 速记符 *(shorthand)* is a single unit of information but formed of 12 characters which, by their fixed and logical features, tend to stay in meaningful groups of syllables that, in other situations, could stand independently: 速记符 (速记+符)

5. STRUCTURE OF INVISIBLE CORE

The *Invisible core* of a unit of information is the inner hidden part carrying the Meaning(s). Depends on the *mono-semantic* or *poly-semantic* feature of the unit, the *Invisible core* can be in single form or the set containing a finite number of meanings.

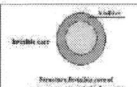

6. STRUCTURE & FUNCTION OF CONTEXTUAL MEMBRANCE

In daily communication, it is rare to exist a *pure unit* of information with only two parts in its structure: *Visibler* and *Invisible core*, but normally goes with *Context*. In other words, unit of information is always covered by the *Contextual membrane*, whose thickness and nature decide the quality of the *Invisible core*, especially with *poly-semantic* units.

There are four possibilities of *Contextual membrane*:

* Firstly, if the *Contextual membrane* is thin, the *Invisible core* of mono- or poly-semantic units is not clear, which leads to the unclearness when the unit comes to human mind.

* Secondly, if the *Contextual membrane* is thick, the *Invisible core* of mono- or poly-semantic units is really clear. However, the ambiguity is remained with poly-semantic units because they have carried different meanings in the core;

* Thirdly, if the *Contextual membrane* is inhomogeneous, the *Invisible core* of poly-semantic units, in this case, still loads more than one meaning, therefore, the ambiguity would happen when these units are perceived;

* Fourthly, if the *Contextual membrane* is homogeneous, the poly-semantic units become mono-semantic ones because the *Invisible core* now remains only one meaning matching the *contextual membrane*.

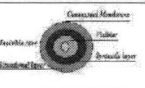

* *Contextual membrane*, in a more detail view, is structured of two layers: *Syntactic layer* and *Situational layer*. Both of them always contain one or more than one but finite number of syntactic (with *Syntactic layer*) and situational features (with *Situational layer*) in each unit of information.

To be continued
Southampton, 04 - 2013

Appendix D: Gold Award Winner Certificate

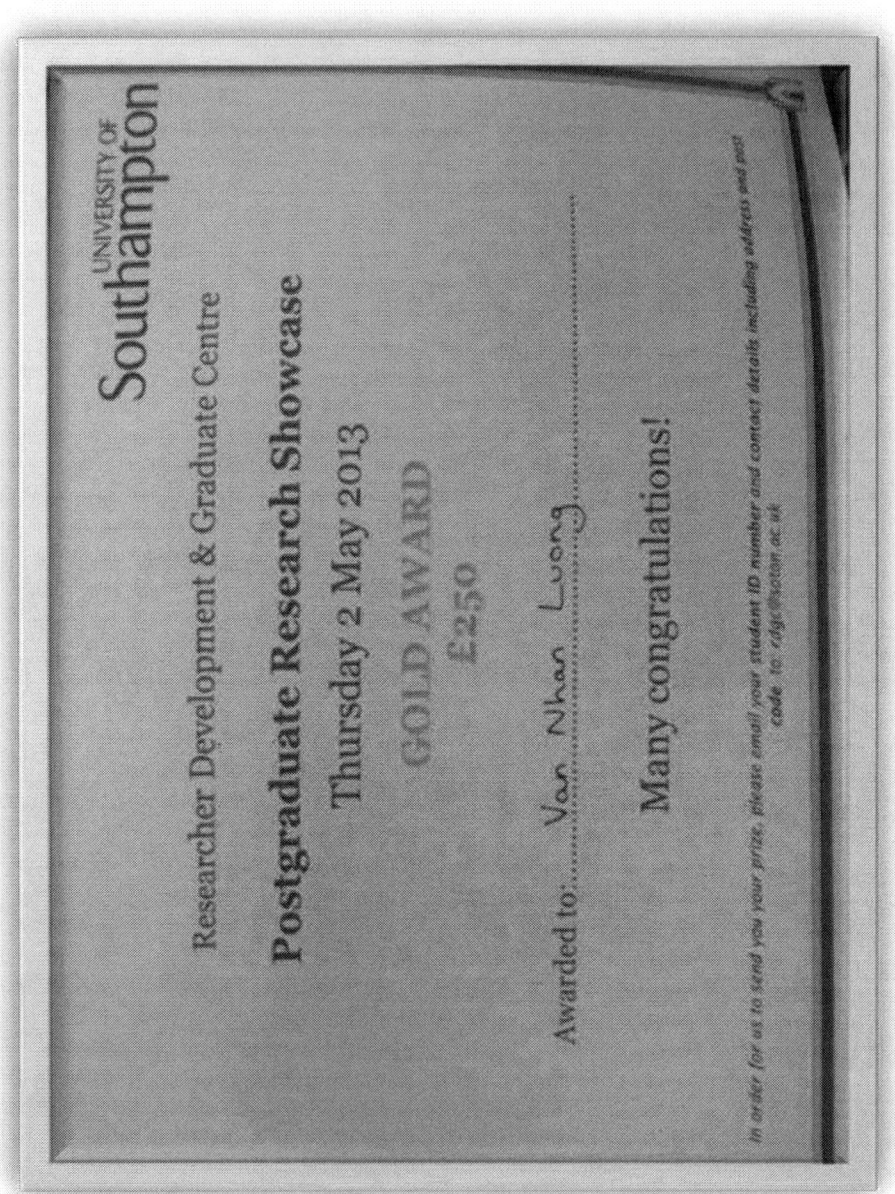

Appendix E: Questions Readers Might Ask

1. Is this book a scientific work or a philosophical speculation?

It is both. The Theory of Continuity is grounded in linguistics, cognitive science, and philosophy. Like Darwin's original theory, it is a framework that can guide future research, not yet a complete body of experimental results.

2. What exactly is the Theory of Continuity in simple terms?

It proposes that knowledge, memory, and identity are built from structured units of meaning. These units can persist beyond one life and reappear in another, just as DNA carries biological information across generations.

3. How does the Theory of Continuity complement rather than replace Darwin's Theory of Evolution?

Darwin explained how bodies form and evolve. The Theory of Continuity explains how meaning and identity may persist. Together, they provide a fuller account of human existence.

4. What is the Atomic Structure in Linguistics, and why is it relevant to the continuity of existence?

It is a model of how meaning is built from *semantic atoms* into larger structures. Because these structures can endure and reappear, the framework explains continuity beyond a single lifetime.

5. Why introduce new terms such as semantic atoms, semantic cores, contextual membranes, and visiblers?

New phenomena require new vocabulary. These terms describe specific mechanisms of meaning-making that cannot be captured with existing words.

6. Are these new terms just metaphors or do they describe real structures?

They describe real structures. Just as atoms were once theoretical but later observed, semantic atoms are proposed as the building blocks of meaning, awaiting empirical confirmation.

7. What kind of evidence supports this theory beyond anecdotes?

The evidence includes cross-cultural cases of children recalling past lives, accounts of acquired savant skills after trauma, and recurrent symbolic motifs across cultures. These are not proofs but patterns that point to structural persistence.

8. How can we test the Theory of Continuity scientifically?

By identifying predictions such as the recurrence of certain semantic cores across unrelated cases, by mapping memory reactivation in neuroscience, and by cross-cultural comparison of symbolic patterns.

9. Is there any link between this theory and current neuroscience or cognitive science?

Yes. Neuroscience shows that memory is reconstructive, not stored as fixed data. This supports the idea of structural reactivation. Cognitive science also confirms that meaning is built from small, combinable units.

211

10. What does this theory say about reincarnation? Does it support it?

It neither confirms nor denies religious reincarnation. It explains observed cases of memory and identity persistence as structural continuity, without invoking a soul.

11. What about people who dismiss reincarnation as a cultural belief or imagination?

The theory recognises cultural influence but shows that some cases go beyond cultural expectations. It treats these cases as structural evidence rather than mystical claims.

12. How does this theory relate to Acquired Savant Syndrome?

It explains the sudden emergence of skills after trauma as the reactivation of latent semantic cores, not random rewiring.

13. Are there parallels between continuity in memory and continuity in language learning?

Yes. Children learn language quickly because they are reactivating structural patterns that pre-exist in latent form.

14. Could cryptomnesia or hidden memory explain these phenomena more simply?

Cryptomnesia explains some cases, but not those with verified details or sudden skills never learned before. Continuity provides a broader explanation.

15. What about cultural conditioning? Could that explain why children recall things from other lives?

Culture shapes expression, but does not explain precise details such as names, locations, or technical skills. Structural continuity accounts for these anomalies.

16. Why should we take unusual cases seriously when they are rare and sometimes controversial?

Science often begins with anomalies. Rare cases of savant skills or past-life recall are valuable precisely because they challenge existing explanations.

17. Is this book proposing a spiritual worldview?

No. It proposes a structural model that can be tested without reference to religion or spirituality.

18. Is there a risk of confusing readers who think this is about religion?

Yes, but the book makes clear that it is not religious. It respects belief systems but stands on scientific and linguistic ground.

19. How is this different from Jung's archetypes?

Archetypes are broad symbolic patterns. The Theory of Continuity identifies specific, structured units of meaning and explains their mechanism of reactivation.

20. How is this different from Dawkins' memes?

Memes depend on imitation and cultural transmission. Semantic atoms are structural, enduring even without imitation.

21. Why should readers trust a linguist to write about neuroscience and philosophy?

Because the theory emerges from linguistics but draws on interdisciplinary evidence, complex questions of continuity require contributions across fields.

22. Is the book too broad, covering too many fields?

It is broad by design. The value of the theory lies in connecting insights from multiple disciplines.

23. What is the main contribution of this book to science and philosophy?

It offers a structural model of continuity, filling the gap between Darwin's biology of formation and the unexplained persistence of meaning.

24. What makes this theory original?

It introduces a linguistic-structural explanation for memory and identity persistence, something not proposed before.

25. What does continuity mean for personal identity? Does it mean "I" survive after death?

Not in a mystical sense. It means that structures of meaning may survive and reappear, though not necessarily the full personal ego.

26. What does this theory suggest about free will?

The Theory of Continuity does not deny free will. It suggests that some of our tendencies, preferences, or symbolic patterns may re-emerge from latent structures carried across lives. However, free will lies in how we respond to these patterns in our present context. Continuity explains the recurrence of meaning, but it does not remove the individual's ability to choose, interpret, and act differently.

27. How does emotion interact with memory in this model?

Emotion encodes memory with intensity, making it more likely to persist and be reactivated.

28. Why is trauma such an important factor in reactivation?

Because trauma creates strong emotional coding, which stabilises semantic cores and makes them more resilient.

29. Can the theory explain déjà vu?

Déjà vu is the sudden feeling that a present situation has already been experienced, even though it is objectively new. The Theory of Continuity explains this as a brief reactivation of latent semantic cores. In such moments, the structural pattern of the experience overlaps with pre-existing structures, creating a sense of familiarity without prior exposure. It is not a literal memory of having been there before, but the re-emergence of a structural pattern that makes the moment feel recognisable.

30. Can the theory explain genius or creativity?

Yes. Genius and creativity can be understood as the reactivation of dense semantic cores. These cores are formed when semantic atoms combine and stabilise, in the same way that chemical atoms merge into persistent compounds in the air. Once formed, these strong cores can exist independently across time. When the right conditions arise, such as trauma, heightened emotion, or altered brain states, the brain can synchronise with these persistent cores and bring them back into activity. This reactivation provides access to knowledge and abilities that seem to appear suddenly, without being learned in the present life.

31. How does the theory view dreams or unconscious thought?

Dreams and unconscious thought can be seen as partial expressions of latent semantic cores. Just as semantic atoms can merge into stable cores that persist across time, these cores may resurface in fragments during sleep or in unconscious processing. The brain, in its resting or altered state, does not always synchronise fully with the core but allows partial reactivation. This creates symbolic images, emotions, or narratives that feel vivid but fragmented. In this sense, dreams are glimpses of deeper structures of meaning that exist independently and occasionally press into awareness when conditions allow.

32. Does this mean that all knowledge is already within us, waiting to be activated?

Not all knowledge exists within us in advance. The Theory of Continuity suggests that some semantic atoms can combine into stable cores that endure across time. These cores may carry knowledge, skills, or symbolic patterns that can be reactivated under the right conditions. However, much of what we know in life still comes from new learning and cultural experiences. Continuity explains why some knowledge appears suddenly or feels strangely familiar, but it does not mean that every possible form of knowledge is already present.

33. Can this theory help us understand education and why some people learn faster?

Yes. Learning is not only the acquisition of new information but also the reactivation of existing semantic cores. When teaching aligns with these latent structures, knowledge feels familiar and is absorbed quickly. This explains why some learners appear to grasp concepts with little effort, while others must build entirely new structures from scratch.

34. What are the practical applications in dementia care?

The theory suggests that even when recent memory fades, older semantic cores may persist. These cores, especially those encoded with strong emotion such as music, ritual, or family bonds, can be reactivated through carefully chosen triggers. Therapies that focus on emotional or symbolic resonance may therefore reach deeper layers of memory and identity, improving quality of life for people with dementia.

35. How could this model be used in therapy for trauma or PTSD?

Trauma can create persistent semantic cores that reactivate repeatedly, producing distressing memories and emotions. The Theory of Continuity explains this as the stabilisation of a strong emotional core that loops back into awareness. Therapy can therefore aim not only at suppressing symptoms but at reframing or gently restructuring the core so that it loses destructive force. This opens the possibility of transforming traumatic memory into new patterns of meaning rather than being trapped by it.

36. Can this theory influence how we design artificial intelligence?

Yes. Most artificial intelligence systems are built to store and retrieve large amounts of data. The Theory of Continuity suggests an alternative model, where systems could be designed to work with structural patterns rather than simple storage. By simulating semantic atoms and cores that can stabilise and reactivate under new conditions, AI could develop more flexible, intuitive, and human-like forms of knowledge processing.

37. What insights could it give into cultural heritage and preservation?

Cultural practices such as rituals, myths, and artistic symbols can be understood as collective semantic cores. These cores persist across generations because they are strongly encoded with emotion and shared meaning. Preserving cultural heritage is not simply keeping records, but maintaining the conditions in which these cores can reactivate and continue to shape identity and community.

38. Is the theory compatible with current evolutionary biology?

Yes. The Theory of Continuity does not replace evolutionary biology but extends it. Darwin explained the continuity of life through biological inheritance. Continuity adds another layer, explaining the persistence of meaning and knowledge through semantic structures. Just as genes carry physical information across generations, semantic cores may carry symbolic information across time.

39. Does it contradict genetics or neuroscience?

No. Genetics and neuroscience explain how the brain and body support memory and learning within a lifetime. The Theory of Continuity recognises these contributions but shows their limits in accounting for knowledge or skills that appear without prior exposure. It adds a structural dimension, suggesting that meaning can persist through semantic cores, complementing rather than contradicting existing science.

40. What do other scholars in linguistics or philosophy think about this idea?

Some may be cautious or sceptical, since the theory moves beyond familiar boundaries. Others see value in its interdisciplinary approach and in its attempt to offer a structural explanation for phenomena that remain unresolved. The theory is best understood as an invitation to dialogue across fields rather than as a final answer.

41. Has the theory been peer reviewed or tested in academic forums?

Parts of the theory have been presented at academic conferences and published in research contexts. The book itself is intended as a broader platform, bringing the framework to a wider audience and encouraging formal review and testing by scholars in different disciplines.

42. How does the author respond to accusations of pseudoscience?

By emphasising that the theory does not claim supernatural forces or untestable beliefs. It is a structural model, like Darwin's theory was at its beginning. It makes predictions about how meaning recurs and can be investigated scientifically. The intention is to open a new line of research, not to close debate.

43. What kind of research should be done next to support this theory?

Future research could include cross-cultural studies that document cases of unusual memory or sudden skills, linguistic analysis of recurring symbolic motifs across societies, and neuroscientific experiments that investigate how memory reactivates under trauma or emotion. Each of these approaches would help to test whether semantic cores behave as the theory predicts.

44. Can ordinary readers understand and apply these ideas to their own lives?

Yes. The theory is written in a way that avoids unnecessary technical detail. Ordinary readers can reflect on their own experiences of memory, intuition, or creativity and recognise them as possible examples of continuity. Teachers, therapists, and carers may also find practical ways to apply the idea of reactivating latent structures in education, wellbeing, or care.

45. Why frame the book as a conversation with Darwin rather than a stand-alone theory?

Because Darwin represents the beginning of a scientific understanding of human life, by presenting continuity as a conversation with him, the book shows that this is not a rejection of his ideas but a continuation. Darwin opened the first chapter by explaining formation; this book opens the next by exploring persistence.

46. What would Darwin himself likely say about this?

Darwin would probably respond with caution but also with curiosity. He insisted that claims should be tested rather than dismissed, and he was willing to follow evidence even when it challenged established beliefs. The Theory of Continuity follows that same spirit by proposing a new framework that invites investigation.

47. Why is the timing right for this book now?

We live in an age when meaning is unstable, shaped by rapid cultural change, digital networks, and global crises. At the same time, new discoveries in neuroscience and cognitive science highlight how memory and identity are more fluid than once believed. This is the right moment to propose a framework that addresses continuity and provides stability in how we understand ourselves.

48. What is the "age of symbolic crisis," and why is it important?

The age of symbolic crisis refers to the present time, when symbols and meanings shift faster than societies can fully absorb them. This creates uncertainty and disconnection. The Theory of Continuity shows that meaning is not endlessly unstable but can persist in stable cores, offering resilience and connection in times of rapid change.

49. How does the theory speak to the future of human knowledge?

It suggests that knowledge does not vanish with the individual but can persist structurally and reappear in new forms.

This means that human knowledge may be less about accumulation and more about reactivation. The future of learning and science could involve recognising these patterns of return and building on them.

50. What is the ultimate message this book wants to leave readers with?

Darwin explained how life begins and evolves, but he left open the question of how meaning and identity endure. The Theory of Continuity proposes that we are not only products of formation but also participants in persistence. Human existence is not only a story of origin but a story of continuity across time.

About the Author

Dr Van Nhan (Adam) Luong is a Vietnamese-born linguist and researcher with over a decade of teaching and research experience at leading UK universities, including Southampton, Liverpool, Durham, Northampton, Huddersfield, Aston, and Birmingham. His expertise covers sociolinguistics, bilingualism, translation, and theoretical linguistics, with a special focus on language, memory, and identity. He developed the award-winning Atomic Structure in Linguistics (ASL), which forms the basis of his Theory of Continuity. His work bridges science and the humanities, offering fresh insights into how knowledge and meaning endure across time. Alongside his academic career, he is the Founder and CEO of the UK–Vietnam Institute of Education Development (UKVIED), which fosters educational collaboration and research partnerships between the UK and Vietnam, and NHAN EDU Ltd, an international education consultancy.